Published by Beautiful Feet Books
1306 Mill Street
San Luis Obispo, CA 93401

www.bfbooks.com
800-889-1978

THE LIFE

OF

GEORGE WASHINGTON.

IN WORDS OF ONE SYLLABLE.

BY

JOSEPHINE POLLARD,

AUTHOR OF "OUR HERO, GENERAL GRANT," "OUR NAVAL HEROES," "THE HISTORY OF THE UNITED STATES," "THE LIFE OF CHRISTOPHER COLUMBUS," ETC., ETC.

NEW YORK:

McLOUGHLIN BROTHERS.

1893

PREFACE.

THE life story of a public man cannot help being to some extent the same thing as a history of the times in which he lived, and to the case of none does this remark apply with more force than to that of the "Father of his Country;" which very title shows the degree to which the personality of its bearer became identified with the public life of the nation. While a great deal of the space in this book, consequently, has had to be devoted to American Revolutionary History, it is hoped that excess in this direction has been avoided, and that the main purpose of the work will be attained, i. e. to give its young readers a distinct and vivid idea of the exalted character and priceless services of Washington, so far as these can be brought within the understanding of a child.

A photographic reproduction of the preface for the 1893 edition.

CONTENTS

PAGE

THE LIFE OF

GEORGE WASHINGTON

CHAPTER 1

BOY-HOOD

GEORGE WASH-ING-TON was born in the State of Vir-gin-i-a, at a place known as Bridg-es Creek, on Feb-ru-a-ry 22, 1732. His great grand-sire, John Wash-ing-ton, came from Eng-land in the year 1657, and took up lands in that state and was a rich man. George was the son of his grand-son Au-gus-tine. Au-gus-tine's first wife was Jane But-ler, who died and left him with two boys. His next wife was Ma-ry Ball, and George was her first child.

The old home-stead in which George was born stood near the banks of the Po-to-mac Riv-er, and was built with a steep roof that sloped down to low eaves that hung out far from the main wall. There were four rooms on the ground floor, and some near the roof, and at each end of the house was a great fire-place built of brick, with broad hearth-stones, such as were in style in those days.

A stone is all that marks the birth-place of George Wash-ing-ton. He was not more than eight years of age when his fa-ther went to live on a farm near the Rap-pa-han-nock Riv-er. The house was built much in the same style as the one at Bridg-es Creek, but it stood on high ground, and here all his boy-hood days were spent.

As there were no good schools in A-mer-i-ca at that time, those who had the means sent their sons to Eng-land to be taught and trained. Law-rence Wash-ing-ton was sent when he was fifteen years of age, and as he was the first-born, it was thought that he would in time take his fa-ther's place, as head of the house.

The school to which George was sent stood in a field on his fa-ther's land, and was taught by a man named Hob-by. This gave it the name of the "Hob-by School."

There were but three things taught there: How to read—How to write—and How to do sums—and some folks thought that these were all their boys and girls had need to learn. Books were scarce and dear, and as most of the men raised fine crops and kept up a brisk trade, they were well pleased to have their boys learn how to buy and sell, and to make out bills. George had been trained by his fa-ther, who was a strict and yet a just man, to love the truth and to do right at all times. He was made to feel that it was a sin to tell a lie, and much worse to hide a fault than to own it.

George had a small axe of which he was quite proud, and boy-like, he cut right and left with it, and thought not of the harm he might do. On the lawn stood a small tree which his fa-ther hoped to see grow up to a good height and to bear fine fruit. George made a great gash in this tree with his sharp axe, and when his fa-ther saw it he was quite sad. He called the boy to his side, and in a stern voice said:

"Who did this? Who cut this tree?"

George hung his head with shame. He knew he had done wrong; and he stood in fear of his fa-ther, who he knew would use the rod where there was need of it. It was a chance for the boy to show what kind of stuff he was made of. George raised his face, still red with the blush of shame, and said in his frank way, and with-out a sign of fear:

"I did it, fa-ther, I can-not tell a lie."

There was no need to use the rod on such a boy as that, and the fa-ther must have felt a thrill of joy when he found that the great truths he had taught his son had such a hold on his mind and had struck their roots deep in-to his heart.

It is told that he clasped George to his breast, and said with tears in his eyes that it would grieve him less to lose scores and scores of trees than to have his boy tell one lie.

But you must not think that George Wash-ing-ton was such a good-good boy that he could guide him-self, and did not need to be kept in check.

He was high strung, as quick as a flash, and felt that he was born to rule, and these traits his mother had to keep down and train so that they would not wreck the young boy, for when George was not yet twelve years of age his fa-ther died, and his mo-ther was left with the care of five young folks. The task was one for which she was well fit, as she had rare good sense, a fine mind, a strong will, and a kind heart.

She used to read to her boys and girls each day out of some good book, talk with them, and tell them how they could best serve God and man, and George laid up each word in his heart, and sought to pay her back as well as he could for all her kind love and care.

She said of George that he was "a good boy"; and it has been said in her praise that "a no-ble mo-ther must have borne so brave a son."

When George was thirteen and his half-bro-ther Law-rence twenty-one, Eng-land and Spain went to war, and Law-rence went with the troops that were sent to the West In-dies. The sight of Law-rence in war-like trim, the sound of drum and fife, and the march of troops through the streets, fired the heart of the young lad, and from that time his plays and games, in school and out, took on a war-like turn.

There was a boy at school, named Wil-li-am Bus-tle, who took up arms and marched with as much zeal as George Wash-ing-ton. But George was at all times com-mand-er-in-chief!

He was fond of all the sports that boys love, and could run, and jump, and climb, and toss bars, and took part in all those feats that kept him in health and strength.

He could pitch quoits with great skill, and the place is shown at Fred-er-icks-burg where, when a boy, he flung a stone a-cross the Rap-pa-han-nock. He was fond of a horse, and there was no steed so wild that George could not mount on his back and tame him.

Mrs. Wash-ing-ton had a colt which she thought so much of that she let it run loose in the field. He was so fierce that no one had dared to get on his back.

One day George went out to view the colt with some of his boy friends, and he told them that if they would help him put the bit in the colt's mouth he would mount. The boys drove the colt in-to a small lot, put the bit in his mouth, and Wash-ing-ton was soon on his back. The beast rushed in-to the field, but was soon curbed by the strong arms of the boy on his back. Then the colt reared and plunged and tried in all sorts of ways to get rid of the lad, who clung to the colt's bare back as if he had been glued there. Mad with rage the colt tried once more to throw him, but strained too hard, and fell to the ground and died in a short time.

The group of boys were well scared at this sad end of their fun, and scarce knew what to do. When they went back to the house Mrs. Wash-ing-ton asked the boys if they had seen her fine breed of colts. "The one I am most proud of," said she, "I am told is as large as his sire." Some of the lads hung their heads and knew not what to say; but George spoke up in his frank way and said that the colt was dead.

"Dead!" cried she; "and from what cause?"

Then George told her just what had been done, and how hard the beast had fought to get free, and how at the last, with one wild fierce plunge, he fell down and died.

A flush rose to the mo-ther's cheek, and then she said to her boy: "It is well; but while I grieve at the loss of my fine colt, I feel a pride and joy in my son, who speaks the truth at all times."

George was fond of his books, too, and was so wise a lad, and so full of thought, and had so keen a sense of what was just, that his school-mates came to him when they got in-to a war of words, or of blows, that he might say which side was right and which was wrong, and thus put an end to the fight. This use of his mind made George look at things in a clear light, and gave him that look of true pride which all men of high mind, the real kings of earth, are wont to wear.

In due time George out-grew the Hob-by School, and was sent to live with his half-bro-ther Au-gus-tine, at Bridg-es Creek, where there was a school of a high grade. But George had no taste for Lat-in or Greek, and liked best to do sums, and to draw maps. He wrote with great care, page after page of what he called "Forms of Writing."

These were notes of hand, bills of sale, deeds, bonds, and the like, such as one would think a boy of thirteen would not care much a-bout.

In this same book (it is kept to this day) George wrote out one hundred and ten "Rules," which were to guide him in act and speech at home and a-broad. Some few of these I will give you, that you may see at how young an age this boy set out to train him-self and fit him-self for the high place he was to fill. It al-most seems as if he must have known the high rank he was to take; but this could not be. His soul was fixed on high things; he had no low tastes; and he was led by the hand of God.

Here are some of the rules that George Wash-ing-ton took as the guide of his youth.

"In the pres-ence of o-thers sing not to your-self with a hum-ming noise, nor drum with your fin-gers or feet.

"Sleep not when o-thers speak, sit not when o-thers stand, speak not when you should hold your peace, walk not when o-thers stop.

"Turn not your back to o-thers when speak-ing; jog not the table or desk on which an-o-ther reads or writes; lean not on a-ny one.

"Read no let-ters, books, or pa-pers in com-pa-ny; but when there is a need for do-ing it, you must ask leave. Come not near the books or wri-tings of a-ny one so as to read them, un-less asked to do so, nor give your o-pin-ion of them un-asked; al-so look not nigh when an-o-ther is wri-ting a let-ter.

"In wri-ting or speak-ing give to each per-son his due ti-tle ac-cord-ing to his rank and the cus-tom of the place.

"When a man does all he can, though it suc-ceeds not well, blame not him that did it.

"Be slow to be-lieve e-vil re-ports of a-ny one.

"Be mod-est in your dress and seek to suit na-ture rather than to win ad-mi-ra-tion. Keep to the fash-ion of your e-quals, such as are civ-il and or-der-ly with re-spect to times and pla-ces.

"Play not the pea-cock, look-ing all a-bout you to see if you be well decked, if your shoes fit well, your stock-ings sit neat-ly, and your clothes hand-some-ly.

"Make friends with those of good char-ac-ter, if you care for your own rep-u-ta-tion, for it is bet-ter to be a-lone than in bad com-pa-ny.

"Speak not of dole-ful things in time of mirth, nor at the ta-ble; speak not of mourn-ful things, as death, and wounds, and if o-thers men-tion them, change, if you can, the dis-course.

"Ut-ter not base and fool-ish things 'mongst grave and learn-ed men; nor hard ques-tions or sub-jects a-mong the ig-no-rant; nor things hard to be be-lieved.

"Be not for-ward, but friend-ly and court-e-ous; the first to sa-lute, hear, and an-swer; and be not pen-sive when it is time to con-verse.

"Gaze not on the marks or blem-ish-es of o-thers, and ask not how they came.

"Think be-fore you speak, pro-nounce not im-per-fect-ly, nor bring out your words too hast-i-ly, but or-der-ly and dis-tinct-ly.

"Treat with men at fit times a-bout bus-i-ness; and whis-per not in the com-pa-ny of others.

"Be not cu-ri-ous to know the af-fairs of o-thers, nor go near to those that speak in pri-vate.

"Un-der-take not to do what you can-not per-form, but be care-ful to keep your prom-ise.

"Speak not e-vil of the ab-sent, for it is un-just.

"Make no show of ta-king great de-light in your food; feed not with greed-i-ness; cut your bread with a knife; lean not on the ta-ble; nei-ther find fault with what you eat.

"When you speak of God, let it be grave-ly and in rev-er-ence. Hon-or and o-bey your pa-rents, al-though they be poor.

"Let your a-muse-ments be man-ful, not sin-ful.

"La-bor to keep a-live in your breast that lit-tle spark of ce-les-ti-al fire, called con-science."

It is not known where George found these rules he took so much pains to write out, but it is plain that he set great store by them, and made use of them through-out his whole life .

CHAPTER II

YOUTH

George was a great pet with his bro-ther, Law-rence Wash-ing-ton, who thought it would be a nice thing for him to serve on board one of the King's ships-of-war. While Law-rence was in the West In-dies he was on good terms with Gen-er-al Went-worth and Ad-mi-ral Ver-non, and he had no doubt they would do their best to get his bro-ther a good place. He spoke to George a-bout it, and the boy was wild with joy. His mo-ther's pride was roused, and at first she did not put a straw in his way, but gave him all the help she could. But as the time drew near, her heart, which had been so strong and brave and full of pride, gave way and she felt that she could not part with her dear boy.

One of her friends wrote to Law-rence that Mrs. Wash-ing-ton had made up her mind not to let George go to sea. She said that some of her friends had told her it was a bad plan, and "I find," said he, "that one word a-gainst his go-ing has more weight than ten for it."

So they gave up the scheme, and George was sent back to school.

He would, on fine days, go out in the fields and tracts of land a-round the school-house, and with line and rod, take the size and shape, the length and width, and mark it all down in one of his books, and so much pains did he take that from the first to the last page not a blot or blur is to be seen.

These neat ways, formed in his youth, were kept up through all his life, and what seems strange is that day-books, and such books as you will find in great use now-a-days were not known at that time. The plan had been thought out by George Wash-ing-ton when a boy of six-teen, and shows the cast of his mind.

Near this time George was sent to live with his bro-ther Law-rence, at his fine place on the Po-to-mac, which he had called Mount Ver-non, to show how much he thought of the ad-mi-ral of that name.

Here George had a chance to make friends with those of high rank, and he spent much of his time with George Fair-fax, who made his home at *Bel-voir,* near Mount Ver-non. Lord Fair-fax, a man of wealth and worth, was much at Bel-voir at that time. He had bought large tracts of land in Vir-gin-i-a, which had not been staked out, or set off in-to lots. In fact, he did not know their size or shape, but he had heard that men had sought out some of the best spots, and had built homes there, and laid out farms for which they paid no rent, and he thought it quite time to put a stop to such things.

In March, 1748, George Wash-ing-ton, who had been picked out by Lord Fair-fax for this task, went on his first trip with George Fair-fax to stake off these wild lands.   He wrote down what was done from day to day, and by these notes we learn that he had quite a rough time of it, and yet found much that was to his taste. He and the men with him rode for miles and miles through lands rich in grain, hemp, and to-bac-co, and through fine groves of trees on the bank of a broad stream.

One night, writes George, when they had been hard at work all day, they came to the house where they were to be fed and lodged. The wood-men went to bed with their clothes on, but George took his off, and as he turned in he found his bed was of loose straw with not a thing on it but the thread-bare blank-et he was to wrap him-self in. The fleas and bugs soon forced George to get up and put on his clothes and lie as the rest of the men did, and "had we not been so tired," he says, " I am sure we should not have slept much that night." He made a vow then that he would sleep out of doors near a fire when on such tramps, and run no more such risks.

On March 18, they reached a point on the Po-to-mac, which they were told they could not ford. There had been a great rain-fall and the stream had not been so high, by six feet, as it was at that time. They made up their minds to stay there for a day or two; went to see the Warm Springs, and at night camped out in the field. At the end of two days, as the stream was still high, they swam their steeds to the Ma-ry-land side. The men crossed in birch-bark boats, and rode all the next day in a rain storm to a place two-score miles from where they had set out that morn. Wash-ing-ton writes that the road was "the worst that had ev-er been trod by man or beast."

On March 23, they fell in with a score or two of red-men who had been off to war and brought home but one scalp, and they had a chance to see a war-dance. The red-men cleared a large space, and built a fire in the midst of it, round which they all sat. One of the men then made a grand speech in which he told them how they were to dance.

When he had done, the one who could dance the best sprang up as if he had just been roused from sleep, and ran and jumped round the ring in a queer kind of way. The rest soon joined him, and did just as he did. By this time the band made it-self heard, and I shall have to tell you what a fine band it was.

There was a pot half full of wa-ter with a piece of deer-skin stretched tight on the top, and a gourd with some shot in it, and a piece of horse's tail tied to it to make it look fine.

One man shook the gourd, and one drummed all the while the rest danced, and I doubt if you would care to hear the noise that was made.

Late in the day of March 26 they came to a place where dwelt a man named Hedge, who was in the pay of King George as jus-tice of the peace. Here they camped, and at the meal that was spread there was not a knife nor a fork to eat with but such as the guests had brought with them.

On the night of the first of A-pril the wind blew and the rain fell. The straw on which they lay took fire, and George was saved by one of the men, who woke him when it was in a blaze.

"I have not slept for four nights in a bed," wrote Wash-ing-ton at this time to one of his young friends at home, "but when I have walked a good deal in the day, I lie down on a heap of straw, or a bear-skin by the fire, with man, wife, young ones, dogs, and cats; and he is in luck who gets the place next the fire."

For three years he kept up this mode of life. As it was a hard life to lead, he could be out but a few weeks at a time. His pay was a doub-loon a day, and some-times six pis-toles.

A doub-loon is a gold coin of Spain, worth not quite six-teen dol-lars. A pis-tole is a small gold coin of Spain, worth not quite four dol-lars.

This rough kind of life, though he did not know it, was to fit him for the toils and ills of war, of which he may have dreamt in those days, as he still kept up his love for war-like things.

While at work on the land round the Blue Ridge, he now and then made his way to *Green-way Court,* where Lord Fair-fax dwelt at this time. Here he had a chance to read choice books, for Lord Fair-fax had a fine mind though his tastes were queer. He lived on a knoll, in a small house not more than twelve feet square. All round him were the huts for his "help," black and white. Red-men, half breeds, and wood-men thronged the place, where they were sure they would get a good meal. He had steeds of fine breed, and hounds of keen scent, for he was fond of the chase, and the woods and hills were full of game.

Here was a grand chance for George, who had a great taste for field-sports, and his rides, and walks, and talks with Lord Fair-fax were a rich treat to the home-bred youth. This wise friend lent George good books which he took with him to the woods and read with great care, and in this way stored his mind with rich thoughts.

In Vir-gin-i-a there were some few men who had served in the late war 'twixt Eng-land and Spain, and they put George through such a drill with sword and with gun that he learned to use them both with great skill.

A Dutch-man, named Van-Bra-am, was one of these men, and he claimed to know a great deal of the art of war. He it was that took George in hand to teach him the use of the sword, and how to fence.

When he was nine-teen years of age, the red-men and the French had made such in-roads on the front that it was thought best to place men on guard to keep back these foes, and to up-hold the laws of the state of Vir-gin-i-a. There was need of some one to take charge of a school-of-arms at one of the chief out-posts where the French sought to get a foot-hold, and the choice fell on George Wash-ing-ton, who set to work at once to fit him-self for the place.

His broth-er's ill health caused this scheme to be dropped for a time, as Law-rence was forced to go to the West In-dies for change of air, and begged George to go with him. George gave up all thought of self, and the two set sail for Bar-ba-does, Sep-tem-ber 28, 1751. At sea he kept a log-book, took notes of the course of the winds, and if the days were fair or foul, and learned all he could of the ways of a ship and how to sail one.

They reached Bar-ba-does on No-vem-ber 3, and were pleased with the place, and all the strange sights that met their gaze. On all sides were fields of corn and sweet cane, and groves of trees rich in leaves and fruit, and all things held out a hope of cure for the sick man, whose lungs were in a weak state. They had been but two weeks in Bar-ba-does when George fell ill with small-pox, and this for a time put an end to all their sports. But he had the best of care, and at the end of three weeks was so well that he could go out of doors.

Law-rence soon tired of this place, and longed for a change of scene. They had to ride out by the first dawn of day, for by the time the sun was half an hour high it was as hot as at mid-day. There was no change in the sick man's health, and he made up his mind to go to Ber-mu-da in the spring. He was lone-some with-out his wife, so it was planned that George should go back home and bring her out to Ber-mu-da.

George set sail, De-cem-ber 22, and reached Vir-gin-i-a at the end of five weeks. He must have been glad to step on shore once more, for the cold winds and fierce storms to be met with at sea, at that time of year, made life on ship-board some-thing of a hard-ship.

Law-rence did not gain in health, and ere his wife could join him he wrote her that he would start for home—"to his grave." He reached Mount Ver-non in time to die 'neath his own roof, and with kind friends at his bed-side. His death took place on the 26th of Ju-ly, 1752, when he was but thirty-four years of age.

He had been like a fa-ther to George, and their hearts were bound by ties so strong and sweet that it was a great grief for them to part.

But George had no time to sit down and mourn his loss. There was work for him to do. New cares were thrust on him by his bro-ther's death that took up all his time and thoughts for some months; and he had to keep up his drills with the men at the school-of-arms, for which he was paid by the State.

CHAPTER III

THE FIRST STEP TO FAME

The time had now come when Wash-ing-ton was to take a fresh start in life and win for him-self high rank.

The French, who thought they had just as good a right as the Eng-lish to take up land in A-mer-i-ca, pressed their claims and built forts on the great Lakes and on the banks of the O-hi-o Riv-er. They made friends of the red-men at or near these posts and made it known that they would fight the Eng-lish at all points.

The red-men on the north shore of Lake On-ta-ri-o were good friends with the French; but those on the south shore were not. They had been well dealt with by the Eng-lish, and their chief, Half-King, did not like the war-like move that was made by the French.

He went to the French post on Lake E-rie and spoke thus to the troops there: "You have no right to come here and build towns and take our land from us by fraud and force. We raised a flame in Mon-tre-al some time a-go, where we asked you to stay and not to come here on our land. I now ask you to go back to that place, for this land is ours.

"Had you come in a peace-ful way, like the Eng-lish, we should have let you trade with us as they do, but we will not let you come and build on our land and take it by force.

"You and the Eng-lish are white. We live in a land be-tween you, to which you and they have no right. The Great Be-ing gave it to us. We have told the Eng-lish to move off, and they have heard us, and now we tell it to you. We do not fear you, and we mean to keep you both at arm's length."

The French-man said to Half-King: "You talk like a fool. This land is mine, and I will have it, let who will stand up a-gainst me. I have no fear of such as you. I tell you that down the O-hi-o I will go, and build forts on it. If it were blocked up, I have troops e-nough to break through it and to tread down all who would try to stop me. My force is as the sand of the sea!"

This proud speech made Half-King feel as if he had been stabbed to the heart. It was the death-blow to his race. But he turned with hope and trust to the Eng-lish, who thus far had not shown a wish to do what was not just to his tribe.

On Oc-to-ber 30, 1753, Wash-ing-ton set out from Will-iams-burg in Vir-gin-i-a with a small band of men. He was just of age and ranked as Ma-jor Wash-ing-ton. He was to go to the French out-post near Lake E-rie, with a note from Gov-er-nor Din-wid-die to the head man there and to ask for a re-ply in the name of King George.

He was to find out where forts had been built and how large a force of troops had crossed the Lakes, and to learn all that he could of those who had dared to set up the flag of France on soil which the Eng-lish claimed as their own.

Wash-ing-ton's route lay through thick woods and swamps where the foot of man had not trod; he had to climb steep and rough hills where wild beasts had their lairs; and to cross streams on frail rafts, if they could not swim or ford them. There were but eight men in the whole band, and

the post they were to reach lay 560 miles off, and the whole of the way had to be made on horse-back or on foot.

They met some of the In-di-an chiefs at a place called Logs-town and Wash-ing-ton made his first speech to the red-men. He told them what he had come for and asked that some of their braves might go with him as guides and safe-guards for the rest of the way. He then gave them what was called a "speech-belt," wrought with beads, as a sign that they were friends and full of peace and good-will.

The chiefs were mild and full of peace. They said that Wash-ing-ton might have some of their men as guides, but he would have to wait for two or three days as the young braves had gone out in search of game.

This Wash-ing-ton could not do. There was no time to lose, and so he set out with but four red-men as guides, and Half-King was one of them.

Through rain and snow, through a long stretch of dark woods that seemed to have no end, through deep streams and swamps where there was no sure foot-hold for man or beast,

the grave band kept on their way. At the end of thirty-five days from the time they left Will-iams-burg, they reached a place called Ven-an-go, where they saw a house from the top of which a French flag flew, and Wash-ing-ton called a halt. The head man in charge asked him and his friends to sup with him. The wine was passed with a free hand, but Wash-ing-ton did not drink like his French host. He knew he would need to keep a cool head for his work. When the French-man had his tongue loosed by the wine, he told a good deal.

"We have got the land," he said, "and we mean to keep it. You Eng-lish may have two men to our one, but you are slow. It takes you a long time to move."

The man's tongue wagged on in a free way, and Wash-ing-ton, who had kept his wits, wrote down all he said that could be of use to him.

The next day it rained hard, and they could not go on. Then for the first time the French-man found that there were red-men with the Eng-lish. Wash-ing-ton had kept them back, for he feared to trust them to the wiles of

the French. But now the shrewd man made a great time, and hailed them as dear friends. He was so glad to see them! How could they be so near and not come to see him? He gave them gifts and plied them with strong drink, till Half-King and his braves thought no more of what they had pledged to the Eng-lish. They were soon in such a state that they did not care to move. It took some time for Wash-ing-ton to get them free from the wiles of the French, and it took four days more of snow and rain, through mire and swamp, to reach the fort for which they had set out.

Here Wash-ing-ton met the chief of the fort and made known the cause that had brought him. He gave him the note from Gov-er-nor Din-wid-die, in which it was asked why the French had come in-to a State that was owned by Great Brit-ain, and they were bid to go in peace. The French took two days in which to think of the course they should take, and in this time Wash-ing-ton set down in his note book the size and strength of the fort and all that he could find out. He told his men to use their eyes and to count the boats in the stream and the guns in the fort.

The first chance he had, Wash-ing-ton drew a plan of this fort, and it was sent to Eng-land for King George to see.

Wash-ing-ton saw that the Half-King and the braves with him had much to say to the French, and he did not trust them. He heard that the Eng-lish who sought to trade on the O-hi-o were seized by the French, and that some red-men had passed the fort with two or three white scalps.

All this made him wish to get off safe with his small band, and when the French chief gave him a sealed note, he had a shrewd guess as to what was in it. At last, when the start was to be made, the French chief had large stores of food and wine put on their boats, and made a great show of good will, but at the same time he tried to keep the red-men with him, and told them he would give them guns for gifts the next day. Wash-ing-ton was pressed by the red-men to wait that long for them, and the next morn the French had to give the guns. Then they tried to get the red-men to drink once more, but Wash-ing-ton plead with them and at last got them to start.

It was hard to steer the boats, as the stream was full of ice, and at times they had to leap out and stand in the wet for half an hour at a time, to drag the boats by main force off the shoals. On the part of the trip that had to be made by land, they had a hard time too. It was cold, the roads were deep in mire, and the steeds were so worn out, that it was feared they would fall by the way. Wash-ing-ton gave up his horse to help bear the food and things for use, and he asked his friends to do so too. They all went on foot, and the cold grew worse. There was deep snow that froze as it fell. For three days they toiled on in a slow way.

At last Wash-ing-ton made up his mind to leave the men and steeds in charge of one of his band, and to strike off with his pack on his back and his gun in his hand by a way which, it seemed to him, would take him home by a short cut. He had the sealed note that he wished to give up as soon as he could. He took but one man with him. At night they lit a fire, and camped by it in the woods. At two in the morn, they were once more on foot.

They fell in with a red-man who claimed to know Mr. Gist, the man who was with Wash-ing-ton, and called him by his name in his own tongue and seemed glad to see him. They asked the red-man if he would go with them and show them a short-cut to the Forks of the Al-le-gha-ny Riv-er. The red-man seemed glad to serve them and took Wash-ing-ton's pack on his own back. Then the three set out and walked at a brisk pace for eight or ten miles.

By this time Wash-ing-ton's feet were so sore that he could not take a step with-out pain, and he was well tired out. He thought it best to camp where they were, and the red-man begged Wash-ing-ton to let him bear his gun. But the Ma-jor would not let it go out of his own hands. This made the red-man cross, and he urged them to keep on and said there were red-skins in the woods who would scalp them if they lay out all night. He would take them to his own hut where they would be safe.

The white men lost faith in their guide and were soon quite ill at ease. When the red-man found that he could not make them go his way or do as he

said, he ceased to wear the face of a friend. At heart he was the foe of all white men. All at once he made a stop, and then turned and fired on them.

Wash-ing-ton found that he was not hit, so he turned to Mr. Gist and said, "Are you shot?"

"No," said Gist. Then the red-man ran to a big white oak tree to load his gun. Gist would have killed him, but Wash-ing-ton would not let him.

Gist says, "We let him charge his gun. We found he put in a ball; then we took care of him. The Ma-jor or I stood by the guns. We made him make a fire for us by a small run as if we meant to sleep there. I said to the Ma-jor: 'As you will not have him killed, we must get rid of him in some way, and then we must march on all night,' on which I said to the red-man, 'I sup-pose you were lost and fired your gun.'

"He said he knew the way to his log-hut and it was not far off. 'Well,' said I, 'do you go home; and as we are tired we will fol-low your track in the morn-ing, and here is a cake of bread for you, and you must give us meat in the morn-ing.' He was glad to get off." Wash-ing-ton says, "We walked all the rest of the night, and made no stop, that we might get the start so far as to be out of their reach the next day, since we were quite sure they would get on our track as soon as it was light."

But no more was seen or heard of them, and the next night at dusk, the two white men came to the Al-le-gha-ny, which they thought to cross on the ice.

This they could not do, so they had to go to work with but one small axe, and a poor one at that, and make a raft. It was a whole day's work. They next got it launched, and went on board of it; then set off.

But when they were in mid-stream, the raft was jammed in the ice in such a way that death seemed to stare them in the face.

Wash-ing-ton put out his pole to stay the raft so that the ice might pass by; but the tide was so swift that it drove the ice with great force. It bore down on the pole so hard that Wash-ing-ton was thrown in-to the stream where it was at least ten feet deep. He would have been swept out of sight if he had not caught hold of one of the raft logs. As they found they could not cross the stream or get back to the shore they had left, they quit the raft and got on a small isle near which they were borne by the tide.

But this was not the end of their ill luck. It was so cold that Mr. Gist's hands and feet froze, and both he and Wash-ing-ton were in great pain through-out the long dark night. A gleam of hope came with the dawn of day, for they found the ice 'twixt them and the east bank of the stream was so hard as to bear their weight, and they made their way on it, and the same day came to a place where they could rest. Here they spent two or three days.

They set out on the first of Jan-u-a-ry, and the next day came to Mon-on-ga-he-la, where Wash-ing-ton bought a horse. On the 11th he got to Bel-voir, where he stopped one day to take the rest he was in need of, and then set out and reached Will-iams-burg on the 16th of Jan-u-a-ry. He gave to Gov-er-nor Din-wid-die the note he had brought from the French chief, showed him the plans of the fort, and told him all that he had seen and done.

The fame of his deeds, of the ills he had borne, and the nerve and pluck he had shown, was soon noised a-broad, and George Wash-ing-ton, though a mere youth, was looked up to by young and old.

CHAPTER IV

TO THE FRONT!

The French chief in his note to Gov-er-nor Din-wid-die had said, in words that were smooth but clear, that he would not leave the banks of the O-hi-o; so the Eng-lish felt as if it were time for them to make a move, though they did not wish to bring on a war.

Land was set off on the O-hi-o where a fort was built, and the rest of it left for the use of the troops.

Wash-ing-ton was asked to lead the troops, but he shrank from it as a charge too great for one so young. So Josh-u-a Fry was made Col-o-nel, and Wash-ing-ton Lieu-ten-ant Col-o-nel of a force of 300 men.

It was hard work to get men to join the ranks. The pay was small, and those who had good farms and good homes did not care to leave them. Those who had a mind to go were for the most part men who did not like to work, and had no house or home they could call their own.

Some were bare-foot, some had no shirts to their backs, and not a few were with-out coat or waist-coat, as the vest was called in those days.

If it was hard work to get this kind of men, it was still more of a task to find those who would serve as chiefs, and Wash-ing-ton found him-self left in charge of a lot of raw troops who knew no will but their own.

But Van-Bra-am, who had taught Wash-ing-ton how to use the sword, was with him, and gave him just the aid he had need of at this time.

On A-pril 2, 1754, Wash-ing-ton, at the head of 150 men, set off for the new fort at the Fork of the O-hi-o. The roads were rough, and the march was slow, and it was not till A-pril 20 that they reached Will's Creek. Here they were met by a small force, in charge of Cap-tain Ad-am Ste-phen. The rest of the force, with the field-guns, were to come by way of the Po-to-mac. These last were in charge of Col-o-nel Fry.

When Wash-ing-ton reached Will's

Creek word was brought him that a large force of French troops had borne down on the new fort. Cap-tain Trent, who was in charge of the few troops in the fort, was a-way at the time, and the young En-sign Ward did not know what to do. He sought the aid of Half-King, who told him to plead with the French, and to beg them to wait till the Cap-tain came back, and the two went at once to the French camp. But the French would not wait, or make terms of peace. They had come as foes, and told En-sign Ward that if he did not leave the fort at once, with all his men, they would put him out by force. All the French would grant was that our men might take their tools with them; so the next morn they filed out of the fort, gave up their arms, and took the path to the woods. The French took the fort and built it up, and called it Fort Du-quesne *(kane),* which was the name of the Gov-er-nor of Can-a-da.

When the sad news was brought to Wash-ing-ton he was at a loss to know what to do, or which way to turn. Here he was with a small band of raw troops right in the midst of foes, red and white, who would soon

hem them in and use them ill if they found out where they were. Yet it would not do to turn back, or show signs of fear. Col-o-nel Fry had not yet come up and the weight of care was thrown on Wash-ing-ton.

He let the Gov-er-nors of Penn-syl-va-ni-a and Ma-ry-land know of his plight, and urged them to send on troops. But none came to his aid.

He had a talk with his chief men, and they all thought it would be best to push on through the wild lands, make the road as they went on, and try to reach the mouth of Red-stone Creek, where they would build a fort. By this means the men would be kept at work, their fears would be quelled, and a way made for the smooth and swift march of the troops in the rear.

There was so much to be done that the men, work as hard as they might, could not clear the way with much speed. There were great trees to be cut down, rocks to be moved, swamps to be filled up, and streams to be bridged. While in the midst of these toils, the bread gave out, and the lack of food made the men too weak to work. In spite of all these ills they made out to move at the rate of four miles a day, up steep hills, and through dense woods that have since borne the name of "The Shades of Death."

While at a large stream where they had to stop to build a bridge, Wash-ing-ton was told that it was not worth while for him to try to go by land to Red-stone Creek, when he could go by boat in much less time.

This would be a good plan, if it would work; and to make sure, Wash-ing-ton took five men with him in a bark boat down the stream. One of these men was a red-skin guide. When they had gone ten miles, the guide said that that was as far as he would go. Wash-ing-ton said, "Why do you want to leave us now? We need you, and you know that we can not get on with-out you. Tell us why you wish to leave."

The red-man said, "Me want gifts. The red-men will not work with-out them. The French know this, and are wise. If you want the red-men to be your guides, you must buy them. They do not love you so well that they will serve you with-out pay."

Wash-ing-ton told the guide that when they got back he would give him a fine white shirt with a frill on it, and a good great-coat, and this put an end to the "strike" for that time. They kept on in the small boat for a score of miles, till they came to a place where there was a falls in the stream at least 40 feet. This put a stop to their course, and Wash-ing-ton went back to camp with his mind made up to go on by land.

He was on his way to join his troops when word was brought him from Half-King to be on his guard, as the French were close at hand. They had been on the march for two days, and meant to strike the first foe they should see.

Half-King said that he and the rest of his chiefs would be with Wash-ing-ton in five days to have a talk.

Wash-ing-ton set to work at once to get his troops in shape to meet the foe. Scouts were sent out. There was a scare in the night. The troops sprang to arms, and kept on the march till day-break. In the mean-time, at nine o'clock at night, word came from Half-King, who was then six miles from the camp, that he had seen the tracks of two French-men, and the whole force was near that place.

Wash-ing-ton put him-self at the head of two score men, left the rest to guard the camp, and set off to join Half-King. The men had to grope their way by foot-paths through the woods. The night was dark and there had been quite a fall of rain, so that they slipped and fell, and lost their way, and had to climb the great rocks, and the trees that had been blown down and blocked their way.

It was near sun-rise when they came to the camp of Half-King, who at once set out with a few of his braves to show Wash-ing-ton the tracks he had seen. Then Half-King called up two of his braves, showed them the tracks, and told them what to do. They took the scent, and went off like hounds, and brought back word that they had traced the foot-prints to a place shut in by rocks and trees where the French were in camp.

It was planned to take them off their guard. Wash-ing-ton was to move on the right, Half-King and his men on the left. They made not a sound. Wash-ing-ton was the first on the ground, and as he came out from the rocks and trees at the head of his men, the French caught sight of him and ran to their arms.

A sharp fire was kept up on both sides. De Ju-mon-ville, who led the French troops, was killed, with ten of his men. One of Wash-ing-ton's men was killed, and two or three met with wounds. None of the red-men were hurt, as the French did not aim their guns at them at all. In less than half an hour the French gave way, and ran, but Wash-ing-ton's men soon came up with them, took them, and they were sent, in charge of a strong guard, to Gov-er-nor Din-wid-die.

This was the first act of war, in which blood had been shed, and Wash-ing-ton had to bear a great deal of blame from both France and Eng-land till the truth was made known. He was thought to have been too rash, and too bold, and in more haste to make war than to seek for peace. These sins were charged to his youth, for it was not known then how much more calm, and wise, and shrewd he was than most men who were twice his age.

The French claimed that this band had been sent out to ask Wash-ing-ton, in a kind way, to leave the lands that were held by the crown of France. But Wash-ing-ton was sure they were spies;

and Half-King said they had bad hearts, and if our men were such fools as to let them go, he would give no more aid.

Half-King was full of fight, and Wash-ing-ton was flushed with pride, and in haste to move on and brave the worst. He wrote home: "The Min-goes have struck the French, and I hope will give a good blow before they have done."

Then he told of the fight he had been in, and how he had won it, and was not hurt though he stood in the midst of the fierce fire. The balls whizzed by him, "and," said Wash-ing-ton, "I was charmed with the sound."

This boast came to the ears of George II, who said, in a dry sort of way, "He would not say so if he had heard ma-ny."

When long years had passed, some-one asked Wash-ing-ton if he had made such a speech. "If I did," said he, "it was when I was young." And he was but twen-ty-two years of age.

He knew that as soon as the French heard of the fight and their bad luck, they would send a strong force out to meet him, so he set all his men to work to add to the size of the earth-work, and to fence it in so that it might be more of a strong-hold. Then he gave to it the name of *Fort Ne-ces-si-ty,* for it had been thrown up in great haste in time of great need, when food was so scant it was feared the troops would starve to death. At one time, for six days they had no flour, and, of course, no bread.

News came of the death of Col-o-nel Fry, at Will's Creek, and Wash-ing-ton was forced to take charge of the whole force. Fry's troops—300 in all—came up from Will's Creek, and Half-King brought for-ty red-men with their wives and young ones and these all had to be fed and cared for.

Young as he was Wash-ing-ton was like a fa-ther to this strange group of men. On Sun-days, when in camp, he read to them from the Word of God, and by all his acts made them feel that he was a good and true man, and fit to be their chief.

The Red-men did quite well as spies and scouts, but were not of much use in the field, and they, and some men from South Car-o-li-na, did much to vex young Wash-ing-ton.

Half-King did not like the way that white men fought, so he took him-self and his band off to a safe place. The white men from South Car-o-li-na, who had come out to serve their king, were too proud to soil their hands or to do hard work, nor would they be led by a man of the rank of Col-o-nel.

In the midst of all these straits Wash-ing-ton stood calm and firm.

The South Car-o-li-na troops were left to guard the fort, while the rest of the men set out to clear the road to Red-stone Creek. Their march was slow, and full of toil, and at the end of two weeks they had gone but thir-teen miles. Here at Gist's home, where they stopped to rest, word came to Wash-ing-ton that a large force of the French were to be sent out to fight him. Word was sent to the fort to have the men that were there join them with all speed.

They reached Gist's at dusk, and by dawn of the next day all troops were in that place, where it was at first thought they would wait for the foe.

But this plan they gave up, for it was deemed best to make haste back to the fort, where they might at least screen themselves from the fire of the foe.

The roads were rough; the heat was great; the food was scant, and the men weak and worn out. There were but few steeds, and these had to bear such great loads that they could not move with speed.

Wash-ing-ton gave up his own horse and went on foot, and the rest of the head men did the same.

The troops from Vir-gin-i-a worked with a will and would take turns and haul the big field guns, while the King's troops, from South Car-o-li-na, walked at their ease, and would not lend a hand, or do a stroke of work.

On the morn of Ju-ly 3, scouts brought word to the fort that the French were but four miles off, and in great force. Wash-ing-ton at once drew up his men on the ground out-side of the fort, to wait for the foe.

Ere noon the French were quite near the fort and the sound of their guns were heard.

Wash-ing-ton thought this was a trick to draw his men out in-to the woods, so he told them to hold their fire till the foe came in sight. But as the French did not show them-selves, though they still kept up their fire, he drew his troops back to the fort and bade them fire at will, and do their best to hit their mark.

The rain fell all day long, so that the men in the fort were half-drowned, and some of the guns scarce fit for use.

The fire was kept up till eight o' clock at night, when the French sent word they would like to make terms with our men.

Wash-ing-ton thought it was a trick to find out the state of things in the fort, and for a time gave no heed to the call. The French sent two or three times, and at last brought the terms for Wash-ing-ton to read. They were in French. There was no-thing at hand to write with, so Van Bra-am, who could speak French, was called on to give the key.

It was a queer scene. A light was brought, and held close to his face so that he could see to read. The rain fell in such sheets that it was hard work to keep up the flame. Van Bra-am mixed up Dutch, French, and Eng-lish in a sad way, while Wash-ing-ton and his chief aids stood near with heads bent, and tried their best to guess what was meant.

They made out at last that the main terms were that the troops might march out of the fort, and fear no harm from French or red-skins as they made their way back to their homes. The drums might beat and the flags fly, and they could take with them all the goods and stores, and all that was in the fort—but the large guns. These the French would break up. And our men should pledge them-selves not to build on the lands which were claimed by the King of France for the space of one year.

The weak had to yield to the strong, and Wash-ing-ton and his men laid down their arms and marched out of the fort.

A note of thanks was sent to Wash-ing-ton, and all his head men but Van Bra-am, who was thought to have read the terms in such a way as to harm our side and serve the French.

But there were those who felt that Van Bra-am was as true as he was brave, and that it was the fault of his head and not his heart, for it was a hard task for a Dutch-man to turn French in-to Eng-lish, and make sense of it.

CHAPTER V

AS AIDE-DE-CAMP

In spite of the way in which the fight at Great Mead-ows came to an end Gov-er-nor Din-wid-die made up his mind that the troops, led by Wash-ing-ton, should cross the hills and drive the French from Fort Du-quesne.

Wash-ing-ton thought it a wild scheme; for the snow lay deep on the hills, his men were worn out, and had no arms, nor tents, nor clothes, nor food, such as would fit them to take the field. It would need gold to buy these things, as well as to pay for fresh troops.

Gold was placed in the Gov-er-nor's hands to use as he pleased. Our force was spread out in-to ten bands, of 100 men each. The King's troops were put in high rank, and Col-o-nel Wash-ing-ton was made Cap-tain. This, of course, was more than he could bear, so he left the ar-my at once, and with a sad heart.

In a short time Gov-er-nor Sharpe of Ma-ry-land was placed by King George at the head of all the force that was to fight the French. He knew that he would need the aid of Wash-ing-ton, and he begged him to come back and serve with him in the field. But Wash-ing-ton did not like the terms, and paid no heed to the call.

The next Spring, Gen-er-al Brad-dock came from Eng-land with two large bands of well-trained troops, which it was thought would drive the French back in-to Can-a-da. Our men were full of joy, and thought the war would soon be at an end. Brad-dock urged Wash-ing-ton to join him in the field. Washington felt that he could be of great use, as he knew the land and the ways of red-men, and so he took up the sword once more, as Brad-dock's aide-de-camp.

Ben-ja-min Frank-lin, who had charge of the mails, lent his aid to the cause, and did all that he could to serve Brad-dock and his men. Brad-dock, with his staff and a guard of horse-men, set out for Will's Creek, by the way of Win-ches-ter, in April, 1755. He rode in a fine turn-out that he had bought of Gov-er-nor Sharpe, which he soon found out was not meant for use on rough roads. But he had fought with dukes, and men of high rank, and was fond of show, and liked to put on a great deal of style.

He thought that this would make the troops look up to him, and would add much to his fame.

In May the troops went in-to camp, and Wash-ing-ton had a chance to learn much of the art of war that was new and strange to him, and to see some things that made him smile.

All the rules and forms of camp-life were kept up. One of the head men who died while in camp, was borne to the grave in this style: A guard marched in front of the corpse, the cap-tain of it in the rear. Each man held his gun up-side down, as a sign that the dead would war no more, and the drums beat the dead march. When near the grave the guard formed two lines that stood face to face, let their guns rest on the ground, and leaned their heads on the butts. The corpse was borne twixt these two rows of men with the sword and sash on the top of the box in which he lay, and in the rear of it the men of rank

marched two and two. When the corpse was put in the ground, the guard fired their guns three times, and then all the troops marched back to camp.

The red-men—the Del-a-wares and Shaw-nees came to aid Gen-er-al Brad-dock. With them were White Thun-der, who had charge of the "speech-belts," and Sil-ver Heels, who was swift of foot. Half-King was dead, and White Thun-der reigned in his stead.

The red-men had a camp to them-selves, where they would sing, and dance, and howl and yell for half the night. It was fun for the King's troops to watch them at their sports and games, and they soon found a great charm in this wild sort of life.

In the day time the red-men and their squaws, rigged up in their plumes and war paint, hung round Brad-dock's camp, and gazed spell-bound at the troops as they went through their drills.

But this state of things did not last long, and strife rose twixt the red and white men, and some of the red-skins left the camp. They told Brad-dock they would meet him on his march, but they did not keep their word.

Wash-ing-ton was sent to Will-iams-burg to bring the gold of which there was need, and when he came back he found that Brad-dock had left a small guard at Fort Cum-ber-land, on Will's Creek, and was then on his way to Fort Du-quesne. He would give no heed to those who knew more of the back-woods than he did, nor call on the red-men to serve as scouts and guides. He was not used to that kind of war-fare, and scorned to be taught by such a youth as George Wash-ing-ton.

The march was a hard one for man and beast. Up steep hills and through rough roads they had to drag the guns, and Brad-dock soon found out that these new fields were not like the old ones on which he had been wont to fight.

Hard as it was for his pride to seek the aid of so young a man, he was at last forced to ask Wash-ing-ton to help him out of these straits.

They had then made a halt at Lit-tle Mead-ows. Wash-ing-ton said there was no time to lose. They must push on at once.

While at this place Cap-tain Jack, and his brave band of hunts-men came in-to camp. They were fond of the chase, and were well-armed with knives and guns, and looked quite like a tribe of red-skins as they came out of the wood.

Brad-dock met them in a stiff sort of way. Cap-tain Jack stepped in front of his band and said that he and his men were used to rough work, and knew how to deal with the red-men, and would be glad to join the force.

Brad-dock looked on him with a gaze of scorn, and spoke to him in a way that roused the ire of Cap-tain Jack. He told his men what had been said, and the whole band turned their backs on the camp, and went through the woods to their old haunts where they were known and prized at their true worth.

In the mean-time Wash-ing-ton, who had had a head-ache for some days, grew so ill that he could not ride on his horse, and had to be borne part of the time in a cart.

Brad-dock—who well knew what a loss his death would be—said that he should not go on. Wash-ing-ton plead with him, but Brad-dock was firm, and made him halt on the road. Here he was left with a guard, and in care of Doc-tor Craik, and here he had to stay for two long weeks. By that time he could move, but not with-out much pain, for he was still quite weak. It was his wish to join the troops in time for the great blow, and while yet too weak to mount his horse, he set off with his guards in a close cart, and reached Brad-dock's camp on the eighth of Ju-ly.

He was just in time, for the troops were to move on Fort Du-quesne the next day. The fort was on the same side of the Mon-on-ga-he-la as the camp, but twixt them lay a pass two miles in length, with the stream on the left and a high range of hills on the right. The plan was to ford the stream near the camp, march on the west bank of the stream for five miles or so, and then cross to the east side and push on to the fort.

By sun-rise the next day the troops turned out in fine style, and marched off to the noise of drum and fife. To Wash-ing-ton this was a grand sight. Though still weak and ill, he rode his horse, and took his place on the staff as aide-de-camp.

At one o'clock the whole force had crossed the ford north of the fort, and were on their way up the bank, when they were met by a fierce and sharp fire from foes they could not see. Wild war-whoops and fierce yells rent the air. What Wash-ing-ton feared, had come to pass. Brad-dock did his best to keep the troops in line; but as fast as they moved up, they were cut down by foes screened by rocks and trees.

Now and then one of the red-men would dart out of the woods with a wild yell to scalp a red-coat who had been shot down. Wild fear seized Brad-dock's men, who fired and took no aim. Those in the front rank were killed by those in the rear. Some of the Vir-gin-i-a troops took post back of trees, and fought as the red-men did. Wash-ing-ton thought it would be a good plan for Brad-dock's men to do the same. But he thought there was but one way for troops to fight, and that brave men ought not to skulk in that way. When some of them took to the trees, Brad-dock stormed at them, and called them hard names, and struck them with the flat of his sword.

All day long Wash-ing-ton rode here and there in the midst of the fight. He was in all parts of the field, a fine mark for the guns of the foe, and yet not a shot struck him to do him harm. Four small shots went through his coat. Two of his steeds were shot down; and though those who stood near him fell dead at his side, Wash-ing-ton had not one wound.

The fight raged on. Death swept through the ranks of the red-coats. The men at the guns were seized in fright. Wash-ing-ton sprang from his horse, wheeled a brass field-piece with his own hand, and sent a good shot through the woods. This act did not bring the men back to their guns.

Brad-dock was on the field the whole day, and did his best to turn the tide. But most of his head-men had been slain in his sight; five times had he been forced to mount a fresh horse, as one by one was struck down by the foe-man's shot, and still he kept his ground and tried to check the flight of his men.

At last a shot struck him in the right arm and went in-to his lungs. He fell from his horse, and was borne from the field. The troops took fright at once, and most of them fled. The yells of the red-men still rang in their ears.

"All is lost!" they cried. "Brad-dock is killed!"

Wash-ing-ton had been sent to a camp 40 miles off, and was on his way back when he heard the sad news.

But Brad-dock did not die at once. He was brought back to camp, and for two days lay in a calm state but full of pain. Now and then his lips would move and he was heard to say, "Who would have thought it! We shall know how to deal with them the next time!"

He died at *Fort Ne-ces-si-ty* on the night of Ju-ly 13. Had he done as Wash-ing-ton told him he might have saved his own life, and won the day. But he was a proud man, and when he made up his mind to do a thing he would do it at all risks. Through this fault he missed the fame he hoped to win, lost his life, and found a grave in a strange land.

His loss was a great gain to Wash-ing-ton, for all felt that he, so calm, so grave, so free from fear, was the right sort of man to lead troops to war. Those who had seen him in the field thought that he bore a charmed life, for though he stood where the shot fell thick and fast he was not hurt, and showed no signs of fear. But Wash-ing-ton was weak, and in need of rest, and as the death of Brad-dock left him with no place in the force, he went back to Mount Ver-non where he thought to spend the rest of his days.

The fight which he took part in as aide-de-camp, and which had so sad an end, goes by the name of *Brad-dock's defeat.*

CHAPTER VI

COL-O-NEL OF VIR-GIN-I-A TROOPS

The troops in Vir-gin-i-a were left with-out a head. There was no one to lead them out to war, and if this fact came to the ears of the French, they would be more bold.

Wash-ing-ton's friends urged him to ask for the place. But this he would not do. His bro-ther wrote him thus: "Our hopes rest on you, dear George. You are the man for the place: all are loud in your praise."

But Wash-ing-ton was firm. He wrote back and told in plain words all that he had borne, and how he had been served for the past two years.

"I love my land," he said, "and shall be glad to serve it, but not on the same terms that I have done so."

His mo-ther begged him not to risk his life in these wars. He wrote her that he should do all that he could to keep out of harm's way, but if he should have a call to drive the foes from the land of his birth, he would have to go! And this he was sure would give her much more pride then if he were to stay at home.

On the same day, Au-gust 13, that this note was sent, word came to Wash-ing-ton that he had been made chief of all the troops in Vir-gin-i-a, and the next month he went to Win-ches-ter to stay.

Here he found much to do. There was need of more troops, and it was hard work to get them. Forts had to be built, and he drew up a plan of his own and set men to work it out, and went out from time to time to see how they got on with it. He rode off thus at the risk of his life, for red-men lay in wait to do deeds of blood.

The stir of war put new life in-to the veins of old Lord Fair-fax. He got up a troop of horse, and put them through a drill on the lawn at Green-way Court. He was fond of the chase, and knew how to run the sly fox to the ground. The red-man was a sort of fox, and Fair-fax was keen for the chase, and now and then would mount his steed and call on George Wash-ing-ton, who was glad to have his kind friend so near.

In a short time he had need of his aid, for word came from the fort at Will's Creek that a band of red-men were on the war-path with fire-brands, and knives, and were then on their way to Win-ches-ter.

A man on a fleet horse was sent post-haste to Wash-ing-ton, who had been called to Will-iams-burg, the chief town.

In the mean-time Lord Fair-fax sent word to all the troops near his home to arm and haste to the aid of Win-ches-ter.

Those on farms flocked to the towns, where they thought they would be safe; and the towns-folks fled to the west side of the Blue Ridge. In the height of this stir Wash-ing-ton rode in-to town, and the sight of him did much to quell their fears.

He thought that there were but a few red-skins who had caused this great scare, and it was his wish to take the field at once and go out and put them to flight. But he could get but a few men to go with him. The rest of the town troops would not stir.

All the old fire-arms that were in the place were brought out, and smiths set to work to scour off the rust and make them fit to use.

Caps, such as are now used on guns, were not known in those days. Flint stones took their place. One of these was put in the lock, so that when it struck a piece of steel it would flash fire, and the spark would set off the gun. These were called flint-lock guns.

Such a thing as a match had not been thought of, and flint stones were made use of to light all fires.

Carts were sent off for balls, and flints, and for food with which to feed all those who had flocked to Win-ches-ter.

The tribes of red-men that had once served with Wash-ing-ton, were now on good terms with the French. One of their chiefs, named Ja-cob, laughed at forts that were built of wood, and made his boast that no fort was safe from him if it would catch fire.

The town where these red-men dwelt was two score miles from Fort Du-quesne, and a band of brave white men, with John Arm-strong and Hugh Mer-cer at their head, set out from Win-ches-ter to put them to rout.

At the end of a long march they came at night on the red-men's stronghold, and took them off their guard. The red-men, led by the fierce chief Ja-cob, who chose to die ere he would yield, made a strong fight, but in the end most of them were killed, their huts were set on fire, and the brave strong-hold was a strong-hold no more.

In the mean-time Wash-ing-ton had left Win-ches-ter and gone to Fort Cum-ber-land, on Will's Creek. Here he kept his men at work on new roads and old ones. Some were sent out as scouts. Brig-a-dier Gen-er-al Forbes, who was in charge of the whole force, was on his way from Phil-a-del-phi-a, but his march was a slow one as he was not in good health. The plan was when he came to move on the French fort. The work that was to have been done north of the fort, by Lord Lou-doun, hung fire. It was felt that he was not the right man for the place, and so his lord-ship was sent back to Eng-land.

Ma-jor Gen-er-al Ab-er-crom-bie then took charge of the King's troops at the north. These were to charge on Crown Point. Ma-jor Gen-er-al Am-herst with a large force of men was with the fleet of Ad-mi-ral Bos-caw-en, that set sail from Hal-i-fax the last of May. These were to lay siege to Lou-is-berg and the isle of Cape Bre-ton, which is at the mouth of the Gulf of St. Lawrence. Forbes was to move on Fort Du-quesne, and was much too slow to suit Wash-ing-ton who was in haste to start. His men had worn out their old clothes and were in great need of new ones, which they could not get for some time. He liked the dress the red-men wore. It was light and cool, and, what had to be thought of most, it was cheap. Wash-ing-ton had some of his men put on this dress, and it took well, and has since been worn by those who roam the woods and plains of our great land.

I will not tell you of all that took place near the great Lakes at this time, as I wish to keep your mind on George Wash-ing-ton.

The schemes laid out by Gen-er-al Forbes did not please Wash-ing-ton, who urged a prompt march on the fort, while the roads were good. He wrote to Ma-jor Hal-ket, who had been with Brad-dock, and was now on Forbes' staff: "I find him fixed to lead you a new way to the O-hi-o, through a road each inch of which must be cut when we have scarce time left to tread the old track, which is known by all to be the best path through the hills." He made it plain that if they went that new way all would be lost, and they would be way-laid by the red-skins and meet with all sorts of ills.

But no heed was paid to his words, and the warm days came to an end. Six weeks were spent in hard work on the new road with a gain of less than three-score miles, when the whole force might have been in front of the French fort had they marched by the old road as Wash-ing-ton had urged.

At a place known as Loy-al Han-nan, the troops were brought to a halt, as Forbes thought this was a good place to build a fort. Some men in charge of Ma-jor Grant went forth as scouts. At dusk they drew near a fort, and set fire to a log house near its walls. This was a rash thing to do, as it let the French know just where they were.

But not a gun was fired from the fort. This the King's troops took for a sign of fear, and were bold and proud, and quite sure that they would win the day. So Brad-dock had thought, and we know his fate.

At length—when Forbes and his men were off their guard—the French made a dash from the fort, and poured their fire on the King's troops. On their right and left flanks fell a storm of shot from the red-skins who had hid back of trees, rocks, and shrubs.

The King's troops were then brought up in line, and for a while stood firm and fought for their lives. But they were no match for the red-skins, whose fierce yells made the blood run chill. Ma-jor Lew-is fought hand to hand with a "brave" whom he laid dead at his feet. Red-skins came up at once to take the white-man's scalp, and there was but one way in which he could save his life. This was to give him-self up to the French, which both he and Ma-jor Grant were forced to do, as their troops had been put to rout with great loss.

Wash-ing-ton won much praise for the way in which the Vir-gin-i-a troops had fought, and he was at once put in charge of a large force, who were to lead the van, serve as scouts, and do their best to drive back the red-skins—work that called for the best skill and nerve.

It was late in the fall of the year when the King's troops all met at Loy-al Han-nan, and so much had to be done to clear the roads, that snow would be on the ground ere they could reach the fort. But from those of the French that they had seized in the late fight, they found out that there were but few troops in the fort, that food was scarce, and the red-skins false to their trust.

This lent hope to the King's troops, who made up their minds to push on. They took up their march at once, with no tents or stores, and but few large guns.

Wash-ing-ton rode at the head. It was a sad march, for the ground was strewn with the bones of those who had fought with Grant and with Brad-dock, and been slain by the foe, or died of their wounds.

At length the troops drew near the fort, and made their way up to it with great care, for they thought the French would be in wait for them, and that there would be a fierce fight.

But the French had had such bad luck in Can-a-da, that they had lost heart, and those in the fort were left to take care of them-selves. So when the Eng-lish were one day's march from the fort, the French stole out at night, got in-to boats, set the fort on fire, and went down the O-hi-o by the light of the flames.

So the fort which had been the cause of so much blood-shed, fell at last with-out a blow, and on No-vem-ber 25, 1758, Wash-ing-ton, with his van-guard, marched in and placed the Brit-ish flag on the wreck of the once proud strong-hold, the name of which was changed to Fort Pitt.

The French gave up all claim to the O-hi-o from that time. The red-skins were quick to make friends with those who held sway, and there was peace with all the tribes twixt the O-hi-o and the Lakes.

Wash-ing-ton had made up his mind to leave the field when this war came to an end, and in De-cem-ber of the same year he bade his troops good-bye.

He had been with them for five years in a hard school, and the strain on his mind had been so great that he lost his health, and felt that he could war no more.

CHAPTER VII

THE HOME OF WASH-ING-TON

In the year 1758, while Wash-ing-ton was with his troops at Win-ches-ter, he met and fell in love with Mrs. Mar-tha Cus-tis. Her home was known as the White House, and here she dwelt in fine style, for she had great wealth. She had a boy six years of age, and a girl of four.

Such were her charms that men of wealth and rank sought for her hand, but Wash-ing-ton, so calm and grave, and with his way yet to make in the world, won her heart, and they were to be wed at the close of the war.

She had heard of the brave deeds he had done, and was proud to be the wife of such a man, so on Jan-u-a-ry 6, 1759, the two were made one.

In the course of a few months Wash-ing-ton went to live at *Mount Ver-non,* where he spent much of his time in the care of his own lands, and those of his wife.

He had a seat with those who made laws for the State, and no man was thought more of than George Wash-ing-ton.

Wash-ing-ton loved to be at *Mount Ver-non,* where he had spent a great part of his boy-hood, with his bro-ther, Law-rence, of whom he was so fond. The house stood on a knoll, and near it were wild woods and deep dells, haunts of the fox and the deer, and bright streams where fish could be found at all times.

His chief sport was the chase, and at the right time of the year, he would go out two or three times a week, with dogs and horns and trained steeds, in search of the sly fox who would lead him and his friends a fine run.

Some times he would go out with his gun and shoot wild-ducks, great flocks of which might be found on the streams close at hand. Or he would scour the woods for the game with which they were filled, and which none but those who owned the place had a right to kill.

A man who had a bad name and paid no heed to the laws that were made, was wont to make his way to the grounds near Mount Ver-non and shoot just what game he chose. More than once he had been told to leave and not come back, but he paid no more heed than if he had been deaf, and was sure to take his pick from the best kind of ducks.

One day when Wash-ing-ton was out on horse-back he heard the sound of a gun down near the edge of the stream. He put spurs to his horse, dashed through bush and brake, and soon came up to the rogue who had just time to jump in his boat and push from shore. Then the bad man raised his gun, cocked it, and took aim at Wash-ing-ton, whom he would no doubt have shot down in cold-blood.

But Wash-ing-ton rode at once in-to the stream, and seized the prow of the boat, and drew it to shore. Then he sprang from his horse, wrenched the gun from the thief's hand, and laid on the lash in such a way that the rogue took to his heels when let loose, and came no more near Mount Ver-non.

As I have told you, men of great wealth dwelt on the shores of the Po-to-mac, and kept house in fine style. They had a large force of slaves, and made great feasts for their friends. One of them used to come out in a rich barge to meet Wash-ing-ton. This barge was rowed by six black men in check shirts and black vel-vet caps.

Wash-ing-ton had a coach and four, with black foot-men, for Mrs. Wash-ing-ton to use when she drove out; but he chose to go on horse-back. Sometimes he and his wife went to An-na-po-lis, to a feast of some sort, where Wash-ing-ton took part.

When storms kept him in the house, he would read, or spend the time at his desk with pen in hand.

He was kind to his slaves, and took the best of care of them when they were sick, but was quick to see that they did not shirk their work. He knew, too, just the kind of work each one was fit for, and which he could do best.

Four of his slaves set out to hew and shape a large log. Wash-ing-ton kept his eye on them and thought they loafed too much. So he sat down, took out his watch, and timed them: how long it took them to get their cross-cut saw and the rest of their tools; how long to cut off the limbs from the tree they had laid low; how long to hew and saw it; what time they spent in talk; and how much work they did while he sat there and took notes. In this way he found out just how much work four men could do in the course of a day— and take their ease.

Wash-ing-ton was quick to lend a hand in time of need, and once when word was brought him that the dam had broke loose, and the mill would soon be swept off, he ran at the head of all his slaves and work-men, and toiled as hard as they in a fierce rain-storm, to check the force of the flood.

The cares of home and state made such calls on his time and thoughts, that he could not be said to live quite at his ease, and he left his mark—a high one—on all that he did.

His crops were of the best, and he sought to cheat no one. The flour he sold from year to year was put up with so much care, and was of such a good kind and so true in weight that all that bore the brand of *George Wash-ing-ton, Mount Ver-non,* was held at a high rate in the West In-di-a ports.

Quite a trade was kept up with Eu-rope, where all the goods had to be bought that were used in the house or on the farm.

Twice a year Wash-ing-ton sent on a long list of such things as he had need of: ploughs, hoes, scythes, horse-goods, and clothes for all the house-hold. For these last he had to give size and height, name, and age, of those who were to wear them.

In one of these lists Wash-ing-ton, who had need of a new suit of clothes, said he was six feet in height, quite thin, and had long limbs. He was then 31 years old.

You will see by what I have told you just how Wash-ing-ton spent much of his time for at least five years. They were five sweet years to him; full of peace, and rest, and joy. He was fond of his home, and felt as much pride in Nel-lie and John Parke Cus-tis as if they had been his own boy and girl. Nel-lie was a frail child, and did not gain in strength, though she had the best of care. Her death took place June 19, 1773, when she was but 17 years of age.

This was a sad blow to Wash-ing-ton, as well as to his wife, and then all their hopes were placed on the son, who bade fair to be a fine strong man. But he died in the year 1781, at the age of 28.

While Wash-ing-ton dwelt in peace at Mount Ver-non, war was rife in the land, but as he had with-drawn from those who bore arms he took no part in it. It was called Pon-ti-ac's war, as it was led by a chief of that name, but the O-hi-o tribes were with him, and the plot was deep laid.

Large tracts of wood-land were laid waste; homes were burnt, and those who dwelt in them robbed and slain; and so sly and shrewd were the red-skins that it was some time ere the white men could put a stop to their deeds of blood.

It was in 1760 that King George the Third made up his mind to tax the folks in A-mer-i-ca for all the goods they bought in Eng-land. The trade was large, and in this way the king could add much to his wealth. But the scheme did not work well. It was first tried in Bos-ton, and set all the folks there by the ears. They claimed that they had rights as well as the king. They had come to this land to be free, and free they would be. They would

do with-out tea and such things, and dress as well as they could in clothes made out of home-made goods.

The king next said that goods bought from Eng-land must bear the king's stamp, for which a sum was to be paid more than the cost of the goods. This was known as the Stamp Act. The folks in A-mer-i-ca were poor. They had not the means to pay this tax. The thought of it filled them with rage; and for five years there was much talk of the wrong the king had done to those who dwelt in A-mer-i-ca.

On the first day of No-vem-ber, 1765, the Stamp Act was to go in-to force, and all New Eng-land was in arms. At Bos-ton bells were tolled; flags were hung at half-mast; shops were shut, and bon-fires built.

In New York, the Act—in clear print—was borne through the streets on a pole, on top of which was a death's head.

A man named Col-den whose place it was to serve out the stamps had to flee to the fort, round which was placed a strong guard from a ship-of-war. The mob broke in-to his coach-house, drew out his coach, put in it a form—stuffed and dressed to look some-what like Col-den—and marched up to the Park where they hung it on a tree.

At night they took the form down, put it in a coach, and bore it back to Bow-ling Green, where the whole thing—coach and all—was burnt right in range of the guns of the fort where the King's troops were.

In March 1766, the king drew back the Stamp Act, which gave great joy to those who had the good of A-mer-i-ca at heart, and to none more than to George Wash-ing-ton. But he made it known that he felt it to be his right as their king to tax them as he chose, and this hurt the pride of those who wished to make their own laws, and be in bonds to no one.

Wash-ing-ton—as did most of those who had Eng-lish blood in their veins—looked up-on that land as his home, and was loath to break the chain that bound him to it. But he did not think well of the Stamp Act, and saw what was sure to come to pass if the king pressed too hard on the A-mer-i-cans.

On Sep-tem-ber 5, 1774, a band of true men from all the States met for the first time in Phil-a-del-phi-a,

and Wash-ing-ton set out from Mount Ver-non on horse-back to take his seat with them. With him were Pat-rick Hen-ry and Ed-mund Pen-dle-ton; and as they rode side by side they talked of the land they loved, and of the hopes they had that all would be well.

The band met with closed doors. Each man wore a grave face. Pat-rick Hen-ry made a strong speech at the close of which he said, "All A-mer-i-ca is thrown in-to one mass. Where are your land-marks? They are all thrown down."

He said he did not call him-self by name of the *State* in which he was born, but by the name of the *land* which gave him birth—then known as *the land of the free.*

Wash-ing-ton was not a man of words, but of deeds. But what he said was of great weight as it came from a wise brain and a true heart.

Pat-rick Hen-ry said there was no man in the whole band so great as George Wash-ing-ton. The band broke up in No-vem-ber, and Wash-ing-ton went back to Mount Ver-non. But not to the gay times and good cheer he once had known. George Fair-fax—who had been his friend from boy-hood—had gone to Eng-land to live, and Bel-voir took fire one night and was burnt to the ground.

The stir in Bos-ton, and in the West where the red-skins were on the war-path, made the whole land ill at ease. Troops were kept on drill, and the roll of the drum was heard in all the small towns. Men came to talk with Wash-ing-ton and to find out what he thought was the best thing to do, and the best way to drill or to arm troops.

It was of no use to plead with the king. He had made up his mind and would not yield an inch. A large force of the best men in Vir-gin-i-a met at Rich-mond, March 20, 1775, and Wash-ing-ton was called on for some plan as to what their course should be.

He told them that he thought there was but one thing to do. Pat-rick Hen-ry put it in-to words that rang through the land: "We must fight! I re-peat it, Sir, we must fight! An ap-peal to arms, and the God of hosts, is all that is left us!"

All hearts were full of zeal; and Wash-ing-ton wrote to his bro-ther, Au-gus-tine, that if there was need of it he would lead troops to war, and risk his life and all his wealth in the cause, which seemed to him a most just one.

CHAPTER VIII

THE BATTLE OF BUNKER HILL

In the year 1775 war was rife in New Eng-land. The King's laws were felt to be more for slaves than for free-men, and all made up their minds to throw off the yoke. They could not bear the sight of the red-coats; and the King's troops were just as fierce in their hate of our men.

Ships-of-war brought a large force of troops to New Eng-land, led by men of rank and fame. They filled the streets of Bos-ton, and it was thought they might bring the A-mer-i-cans to terms, and not a drop of blood be shed. But this was not to be.

A large force of our men were in camp on the hills and fields near Bos-ton, the sight of whom might well cause the well-clad Brit-ish to smile. They had left their farms in great haste at the cry of "To arms!" had seized their guns, and come in the home-spun clothes it was their pride to wear. Those from Mas-sa-chu-setts were led by Gen-er-al Ar-te-mas Ward; those from New Hamp-shire by Col-o-nel John Stark; those from Rhode Isl-

and by Gen-er-al Na-than-iel Greene; and those from Con-nect-i-cut by Gen-er-al Is-ra-el Put-nam; all brave and true men, and full of fight.

But the troops had need to be well armed; and all the guns and such things as there was need of in war times were in Bos-ton, where the red-coats were on guard. But though sharp eyes were on the watch, sly deeds were done by those who knew the ways in and out of each store-house. Carts went out of town heaped high with dirt in which guns and balls were hid; and all sorts of tricks were used to get such things past the red-coats.

At length it came to the ears of Gen-er-al Gage, that some field guns were at Sa-lem, and he sent troops there to seize them. But when they reached Sa-lem they found no guns there.

Then word came to Gen-er-al Gage that there was a large stock of arms and war-stores in Con-cord, which was less than a score of miles from Bos-ton.

In the night of A-pril 18, the red-coats set out for Con-cord. Gen-er-al

Gage had said that no one but the troops should leave the town, but the news was borne to Lex-ing-ton—a town on the road to Con-cord—by those who were as swift as the hare, and as sly as the fox.

The folks there met in groups, with hearts on fire. Bells were rung and guns were fired. Men who heard these sounds ran as fast as they could to Lex-ing-ton, to hold the bridge, and keep back the foe.

At five o'clock, on the morn of A-pril 19, the red-coats came in sight, and at once three-score and ten men stood out on the green near the wall to meet them.

Ma-jor Pit-cairn who was at the head of the King's troops called out to these brave men to lay down their arms and leave the place. But they paid no heed to his words. Then he sprang from the ranks, shot off a small gun, swung his sword in air, and told his men to fire. The troops ran up, with loud cheers, and poured a storm of shot on our men, some of whom were killed. Then they pushed on to Con-cord, and did all the harm they could at that place: spiked guns, threw pounds and pounds of shot

down the wells, and spoiled a large lot of flour and food that had been stored there for use in time of need.

When the King's troops turned back to Lex-ing-ton, they were quite worn out with what they had done, and would have been cut down by our men if Gage had not sent a force to their aid.

For the blue-coats had flown to arms, and poured in-to Lex-ing-ton by all the roads that led there-to. The red-coats might laugh at their clothes, and the way in which they tried to keep step, but they found out that they knew how to use guns, and that each man was a dead-shot.

The fresh troops Gage sent up from Bos-ton had to form a square, so that the worn out men who had had a long march and hard work might have a chance to rest. Then they all set out to march back to Bos-ton, with two field guns in the rear to keep off the "flock of Yan-kees," who dogged their steps, and kept up a fire in front and rear, and from each stone-wall and hedge that lined the road.

There was loss on both sides, but what hurt the King's troops the most was to be put to flight by such

a lot of scare-crows, as they thought our troops were.

A close watch was kept on Bos-ton by our men, who were soon in such force that it would not have been safe for the red-coats to try to leave the town. The King's troops did not like to be shut in, in this way, and lost no chance to mock at and taunt those who kept them at bay.

On the north side of Bos-ton lay a long strip of land, from the heights of which one could see the town and all the ships at or near the wharves. Put-nam thought it would be a good plan to seize these heights and place troops there; but Ward and War-ner thought it was not safe to risk it. It might bring on a fierce fight and cause much blood to be shed.

Put-nam had no fear of his own men. He knew how brave they were, and how well they could fight back of a screen. "They have no fear of their heads," he said, "their chief thought is their legs. Shield them, and they'll fight on till doom's day."

Two or three of those who had led troops in the French war, were of the same mind as Put-nam, and their words had weight. The chief man was Col-o-nel Pres-cott, who was just the style of man, in port and in dress, that a lot of raw troops would look up to. He wore a fine hat, a top-wig, and a blue coat faced and lapped up at the skirts.

He it was whom Gen-er-al Ward chose to lead the troops which were to seize the heights, build the earth-works there, and guard them from the foe. There were 1200 in all, and they set out on the night of June 16, 1775. Not a light was shown. Not a sound was heard, but the tramp—tramp—tramp of these men on their way to face death.

A small neck of land joined Charles-town to the main-land, and as they drew near this the troops hushed their steps, and moved with great care. For on this the red-coats kept a close watch. Five of their ships-of-war stood so that their guns would sweep this neck of land, and earth-works were on Copp's Hill, which faced Charles-town.

On the blue-coats went, past the guards, past the guns, past the Neck, and up to the heights of Bunk-er's Hill. Here they were to make their stand, but it was found that Breed's

Hill, which was half a mile off, was not quite so steep, and would give them more of a chance at the red-coats, while Bunk-er's Hill would shield them in the rear.

Put-nam thought Breed's Hill was the right place and was in haste for the work to go on. There was no time to lose. So pick and spade were brought out, and the earth dug out so as to serve as a wall to screen them from the fire of the foe.

The night was warm and still. Now and then Pres-cott would steal down to the edge of the stream, to see and hear if the red-coats had made a stir. There was not a sound save the cry of "All's well! All's well!" from the watch-man on guard in the town, and on the ships-of-war.

All night the work on the heights went on. At dawn of day the men there were seen by the sea-men on the ships-of-war, and at once their guns were brought up and turned on the hill. Their shot did not harm the works, but one man who went out-side was killed, and this threw the rest in-to a great fright. They were not used to scenes of war, and the sight of a man shot down in their midst was more than their nerves could stand.

Some took to their heels at once, and did not come back, and had Pres-cott not been a brave man him-self he could not have held his troops as he did. He stood up on top of the earth-works in full view of the red-coats, and talked with his men, and his words of cheer put new strength in their hearts, so that they were in less dread of the balls that whizzed near them.

The noise of the guns roused the red-coats in Bos-ton, and Gen-er-al Gage gazed at Breed's Hill like one in a dream. A fort full of men had sprung up in the night! How had it been done? What kind of men were these he had to meet? As he stood on Copp's Hill and looked through his field glass, he spied the tall form of Pres-cott, in his blue coat, on the wall of the fort.

"Will he fight?" asked Gage, "Yes, *sir,*" said one who stood near, and who knew Pres-cott. "He will fight to the last drop of blood; but I can't say as much for his men."

"We must seize the works!" cried Gage, and at once called up his chiefs for a talk, and to plan the best way to do this deed.

The noise in the streets of Boston, the roll of the drum, the sound of the trump that calls to war, the sharp click of hoofs, and the deep roll of wheels that bore the field guns, were heard on the heights, and let the troops there know that war was at hand.

The men were worn out with their hard task, and their loss of sleep. They had not brought much food with them, and their thirst was great. The heat made them feel weak and dull. There was need of more men, and a lot of raw New Hamp-shire troops, led by Col-o-nel Stark came to their aid. In the meantime those on the height had to bear the fire of the guns from the ships and from Copp's Hill, which broke on them at ten o'clock.

At noon the blue-coats saw more than a score of boats full of troops cross from Bos-ton in straight lines. The sun shone on their red-coats, and flashed from the tips of the guns they bore, and from the brass field guns that stood on the deck. It was a gay scene. They made their way to a point north of Breed's Hill, where Gen-er-al Howe, who led them, could see the full strength of the blue-coats. They had more troops than he thought, and he caught sight of fresh ones on their way to Breed's Hill.

Howe at once sent to Gage for more troops, and more balls for the field guns, and as it would take some time for them to be sent round, the red-coats in the mean-time were served with food and drink. The "grog" was passed round in pails, and the men sat round on the grass, and ate and drank their fill, while the poor men on the heights looked down and longed to share their feast.

But while the red-coats took their ease, the blue-coats had a chance to add to the strength of their fort, and to push out the breast-works to a point known as the Slough.

Near this was a pass where the foe might turn the left-flank of the troops or seize Bunk-er's Hill.

Put-nam chose one of his men, a Cap-tain Knowl-ton, to hold this pass with his Con-nect-i-cut troops. He at once set to work to build a sort of fort, back of which his men could fight with more ease than if they stood out in the field. Not a long way off was a post-and-rail fence set in a low foot-wall of stone, and this fence ran down to the Mys-tic Riv-er. The posts and rails of a fence, near this, were torn up in haste, and set a few feet at the rear of it, and the space 'twixt the two was filled with new-mown hay brought from the fields near at hand.

While Knowl-ton and his men were at work on this fence, Put-nam and his troops threw up the work on Bunk-er's Hill.

In the mean-time Stark had set out from Med-ford on a six mile march. He was a cool, calm man, and had been through the French war, of which I have told you. He led his men at a slow pace, so that they would be fresh and strong to take part in the fight. As they came up to the Neck, which they had to cross, and which was lined with guns on both sides, one of the aides urged him to let the men take a quick step.

The old man shook his head, and said, "One fresh man in a fight is worth ten tired ones," and kept on at the same pace; and did good work that day back of the post-and-rail screen.

War-ren, who had been made a Ma-jor Gen-er-al, came to serve in the ranks. Put-nam said he might lead the troops at the fence. He said he did not care to lead; he was there to fight. "Where will the fire be the hot-test?" he asked. He was told that the fort on Breed's Hill was the point the foe sought to gain. "If we can hold that," said Put-nam, "the day is ours."

War-ren at once made his way there, and the troops gave a round of cheers when he stepped in-to the fort. Pres-cott, who was not so high in rank, sought to have War-ren take charge of the troops. But he would not. "I have come to serve in the ranks," he said, "and shall be glad to learn from one so well-skilled as your-self."

The red-coats thought to take the works with ease, and win the day. Gen-er-al Pig-ot, with the left wing, was to mount the hill and seize the earth-works, while Gen-er-al Howe came up with the right wing to turn the left-flank of our men and stop all flight at the rear.

Pig-ot and his men came up the height, and not a gun was fired by our troops till the red-coats were in range.

Then, as they were all good marks-men each shot told, and some of the best men fell at the first fire. The foe fell back in haste, but were brought up once more by those who stood at their head with drawn swords.

They were met by a fire more fierce than the first, and vexed by the guns that bore on their flank from the band of men in Charles-town. So much blood had been shed, and the men were in such a state of fright, that Pig-ot was forced to give the word to fall back.

We will now see what sort of luck Gen-er-al Howe had. He led his troops up the bank of the stream, and thought to take the slight breast-work with ease, and so get in the rear of the fort. But he did not know the ground, and could not bring his large guns through the swamp he met with. In the pause some of his men were hurt and some killed by the guns that were set by the post-and-rail fence.

Howe's men kept up a fire as they came on, but as they did not take good aim the balls flew o'er the heads of our troops, who had been told to hold their fire till the red-coats were quite near.

Some few did not do as they were told, and Put-nam rode up and swore he would cut down the next man that fired ere he had the word to do so. When the red-coats were in the right range, such a storm of lead poured on them from guns in the hands of men who did not miss a mark that the place was like a field of blood.

Such a host were slain that the red-coats lost heart, and fell back in great haste. Some of them ran back as far as the boats, and got on board of them that they might be safe from the fire of the marks-men.

Once more the red-coats charged the fort, which it was their aim to get in-to their own hands. In the mean-time the shells from Copp's Hill and the ships-of-war had set Charles-town on fire. The town was built of wood, and was soon a mass of flames. The dense smoke put out the light of the sun. On all sides was heard the din of war. The big guns kept up their great roar. Bomb-shells burst in the air. The sharp hiss of the small balls, and the shouts and yells of the men made a scene to strike the heart with awe.

Our men stood firm, and with eyes fixed on the foe, who, as soon as they were close at hand, were shot down by the guns whose aim was so sure.

The red-coats stood the first shock, and then kept on, but were met by such a stream of fire that they were soon brought to a halt. In vain did the men who led them urge them on with drawn swords. Whole ranks were mowed down. Some of Gen-er-al Howe's staff were slain, and the troops, wild with fear, broke ranks and fled down the hill.

For a third time Gen-er-al Howe brought up his men, some of whom threw off their knap-sacks and some their coats that they might not be weighed down by them.

The red-coats made a feint as if they would take the fort at the fence, and did much harm there to our men. While some of his troops were at work at that point, Howe brought the rest of his force to the front and rear of the main fort, which was then stormed on three sides at once.

Pres-cott told some of his men to stand at the back part of the fort and fire at the red-coats that showed them-selves on the wall. Soon one leaped up and cried out "The day is ours!"

and was shot down at once, as were all those who had joined him.

But our men had fired their last round, and there was nought for them to do but to meet the foe in a hand-to-hand fight. With stones and the butt-ends of their guns they sought to drive back the red-coats, but the tide was too strong for them, and they had to give way.

War-ren, who had done brave work that day, was the last to leave the fort. He scarce had done so ere he was struck by a ball and fell dead on the spot.

As our troops fled by way of Bunk-er Hill, Put-nam ran to the rear and cried, "Halt! make a stand here! We can check them yet! In God's name form, and give them one shot more!"

But the troops could not be brought to a stand, and the red-coats won the day, but with the loss of more than half of their men. And it hurt their pride to think that it had cost them so dear to take these earth-works that had been thrown up in one night by a mere hand-ful of raw troops.

Their loss was 1,054.

Our loss was 450.

CHAPTER IX

COMMANDER—IN—CHIEF

The deeds done ere this by the King's troops had made a great stir through-out the land. The chief men of each State met in Phil-a-del-phi-a, and sought out ways and means to help those who were in arms, as foes of King George, and a large force of men, from Ma-ry-land, Penn-syl-va-ni-a, and Vir-gin-i-a, were soon on hand to march and join the troops near Bos-ton.

But who was to lead them? The choice at once fell on George Wash-ing-ton, but he held back. He thought that Mas-sa-chu-sett's troops might not care to be led by a man from the south; and, too, Gen-er-al Ward, who was then at their head had the first right, for Wash-ing-ton's rank was not so high as his.

There was much talk on this score, and in the midst of it a Mas-sa-chu-setts man, John Ad-ams, rose and said that the man he thought fit to lead our troops was in that room, and he came from Vir-gin-i-a.

All knew whom he meant, and as Wash-ing-ton heard his own name he rose from his seat and left the room.

Then votes were cast, and all were for Wash-ing-ton, and he felt that he could not say "No" to such a call. He spoke his thanks in a few words, and said that he would do the best that he could, and serve with-out pay. He set out from Phil-a-del-phi-a June 21, 1775. With him were Gen-er-al Lee and Gen-er-al Schuy-ler, and a troop of light-horse, which went all the way to New York.

As soon as it was known that Wash-ing-ton was on the road, crowds ran out to meet him, and to show their pride in him.

When he reached New York he heard of the fight at Bunk-er Hill, and made haste to join the troops in their camp at Cam-bridge. He reached there Ju-ly 2. The next day all the troops were drawn out in line, and Wash-ing-ton rode out at the head of his staff till he came to a large elm tree. Here he wheeled his horse, and drew his sword and took charge of all

our troops as their Com-mand-er-in-chief.

He found much to do, and much to bear from his own men as well as from the red-coats. It came to his ears that our men who fell in-to the hands of the red-coats at Bunk-er's Hill, were not well used, and he wrote at once to Gage and asked him to be less harsh. Gage, who had fought by his side in 1753, when both were young men, wrote back that he thought he should have praise and not blame, since he had saved the lives of those who were doomed to be hung.

Wash-ing-ton at first thought he would do as he was done by, but his heart failed him, and those of the red-coats that were in the hands of our troops were set free, if they gave their word they would not fight for King George.

By such acts Wash-ing-ton sought to show that "A-mer-i-cans are as mer-ci-ful as they are brave."

The camps in which Wash-ing-ton found his troops were as odd as the men them-selves. Some of the tents were made of boards, some of sail-cloth, or bits of both, while here and there were those made of stone and turf, brick and brush-wood. Some were thrown up in haste and bore no marks of care, while a few were wrought with wreaths and twigs, and spoke well for the taste of those who made them.

The best camp of all was that of the Rhode Is-land men in charge of Gen-er-al Na-than-i-el Greene. Here were found as good tents as the red-coats had, and the men were well-drilled and well-dressed. Greene was brought up on a farm. His fa-ther was a black-smith, and at times his son worked with the plough, or took his place at the forge.

At the first note of war, Greene left the farm and in the month of May, 1775, was in charge of all the troops of his own small state. He went to Bos-ton, and took notes while there of all that the red-coats did, and in this way learned much that he could put to good use. His troops had fought at Bunk-er Hill, and there were none in the whole force that bore them-selves so well, or made so fine a show.

Greene was six feet tall, and not quite two score years of age. He was strong and well built, and his frank way won the heart of Wash-ing-ton, and the two were warm friends from that time.

Wash-ing-ton now set to work to add strength to the weak parts of his line, and to throw up fresh works round the main forts. All the live stock had to be kept off the coast so that they would not fall in-to the hands of the foe.

He sought to draw the red-coats out of Bos-ton, but they would not stir. When Wash-ing-ton took charge of the troops, he thought that he could go back to his home when the cold days came on, and spend some time there with his wife.

But there was no chance for him to leave, so he wrote to Mrs. Wash-ing-ton to join him in the camp. She came and stayed with him till the next spring; and this was her course all through the war.

She came in her own coach and four, with her son and his wife. The black foot-men were dressed in red and white, and the whole turn-out was in the style in use in Vir-gin-i-a at that day.

Wash-ing-ton had his rooms in the Crai-gie House, in Cam-bridge, and here Mrs. Wash-ing-ton took charge

and gave the place more of a home-like air.

At that time the camp of Cam-bridge was filled with all sorts of troops. Some had spent the most of their lives in boats, some were brought up on farms, some came from the woods, and each group wore the dress that pleased them best, and laughed at those who were not dressed the same.

This made sport for some time and jokes flew thick and fast.

One day some men came in-to camp dressed in an odd garb, such as was worn to hunt in. The suit was made of deer-skin, and the long shirt had a deep fringe all round. This dress was the cause of much mirth to men who came from the sea-shore, and were used to short coats, and rough plain clothes.

There was snow on the ground, and when the jokes gave out, snow-balls took their place, for a war of words is quite sure to end in blows. Men came up to the aid of both sides. Fists were used, and all took part in the hand-to-hand fight, and there was a great stir in the camp.

While the fight was at its height Wash-ing-ton rode up. None of his aides were with him. He threw the reins of his own horse in-to the hands of the black-man who rode near, sprang from his seat, and rushed in-to the thick of the fray. Then he seized two of the tall stout hunts-men by the throat, and talked to them and shook them while he held them at arm's length.

This put an end to the brawl at once, and the rest of the crowd slunk off in haste, and left but three men on the ground: Wash-ing-ton, and the two he held in his grasp.

As the cold days and nights came on the men grew home-sick, and longed to be by their own fire-sides. It was right that some of them should go, for they had served out their time, and this made the rest lone-some and sad. Songs would not cheer them, and they paid no heed to the words of those who sought to rouse them from these depths of woe.

Wash-ing-ton was full of fears, which were shared by all those who were near him in rank, yet he did not lose hope. Gen-er-al Greene wrote, "They seem to be so sick of this way of life, and so home-sick, that I fear a large part of our best troops will soon go home." Still his heart did not lose hope. All would come right in time; and his words of cheer were a great help to Wash-ing-ton at this time.

The year 1775 had been a dark one for our land, and there was no ray of hope to light the dawn of 1776. There were but 10,000 troops to take the field. There was a lack of arms, a lack of clothes, and a lack of food, and these things made camp-life hard to bear, and were a great grief to the heart of the chief. He could not sleep. Had the foe known of their plight, they would have borne down on them and swept them out of sight. But God took care of them.

In the first month of the year there was a stir on the Bos-ton wharves. A large fleet of boats lay in the stream, on board of which the red-coats swarmed, and there were two sloops-of-war filled with guns and war-like stores.

All were in charge of Gen-er-al Howe, and Wash-ing-ton guessed what his plans were, and felt that the time had come for him to strive to wrest Bos-ton from the King's troops.

The out-look was bright. More troops had come to his aid, and he made up his mind to place part of his force on Dor-ches-ter Heights, and, if he could, draw out the foe to fight at that place. At a sign, the troops on the Heights and at Nook's Hill were to fire at the same time, and rake the town with balls and bomb-shells. At the same time boats full of troops were to start from the mouth of Charles River, and act in the rear of the red-coats. It was thought that these moves on the part of our troops would bring on such a fight as they had had on Breed's Hill.

On the night of March 4, our men made their way to the Heights, and at dawn of the next day strong forts loomed up, and seemed as if they must have been brought there at the touch of a wand.

Howe gazed on them and said, "The reb-els have done more work in one night than my whole ar-my would have done in a month."

He must drive them from the Heights, or leave Bos-ton. While pride urged him on, fear held him back, for he knew that his loss would be great. But he must make a move of some sort, so he made up his mind to send boats out that night with a force of troops in charge of Lord Per-cy. But a storm came up from the east; the surf beat high on the shore where the boats would have to land; and the scheme was put off till the next day. But it stormed just as hard the next day; the rain came down in sheets; and the boats stayed where they were.

In the mean-time our men kept at work on the hills on the north-side and south side, and when the storm ceased Gen-er-al Howe saw that the forts were now so strong there would be no chance to take them.

Nor was it safe for him to stay in Bos-ton. Yet the Ad-mi-ral said that if Howe's troops did not seize the Heights, the ships-of-war should not stay near Bos-ton; so his lord-ship would have to leave with what grace he could, much as it might wound his pride.

When the word went forth that the troops were to leave, strange sights were seen in Bos-ton town and bay. For some days the red-coats went this way and that in great haste. More than three-score-and-ten boats were cast loose for sea, with at least 12,000 men on board of them. While this stir took place not a shot was sent from the Heights, and it was well that this was so, as the red-coats had laid plans to set the town in a blaze if our troops fired one gun.

The red-coats left Bos-ton March 17, and our troops, in charge of "Old Put"—as the brave Put-nam was called—marched in-to town in fine style.

For some days the fleet lay off the coast of Rhode Isl-and, and it was feared for a-while that they meant to strike a blow and win back what they had lost. But no such thing took place, ere long the fleet sailed out of sight.

"Where they are bound," wrote Wash-ing-ton, "and where they next will pitch their tents, I know not."

He thought they were on their way to New York, but such was not the case. They had steered for Hal-i-fax, to wait there for more troops, and for the large fleet that was to come from Eng-land.

A vote of thanks and a large gold coin with his face on one side of it, were sent to Wash-ing-ton by the chief men of the land, as part of his due for what he had so far done to save A-mer-i-ca from King George's rule.

Wash-ing-ton, who thought the next move of the red-coats would be on New York, set out for that place, and reached there A-pril 13. He went to work at once to build forts, and to send out troops, and to make the place as strong as it ought to be. He did not know the plans of the foe, nor from what point they would hurl the bolts of war.

All was guess-work, but still in the midst of doubt it would not do to be slack.

The town was put in charge of the troops, and the rules were quite strict. Those who went in or out had to give the pass-word. "We all live here, shut up like nuns," wrote one who was fond of a gay life. "There's no one in town to see, and none to come to see us."

Good times in New York were at an end. Our troops had been forced to leave Can-a-da, and it was known that the red-coats would push their way to New York. Forts were built on high banks up the Hud-son, and on the isles at its mouth, and all done that could be done to check them in their march.

In the mean-time it had been thought a good plan to set a day in which it might be shown through-out the land that A-mer-i-ca was, and, of a right, ought to be, a free land. So in Ju-ly an Act was drawn up and signed by the wise men who met in Phil-a-del-phi-a to frame the laws for the new States, and there was great joy, for it was a great day.

Bells were rung. Shouts and cheers rent the air. Fires blazed, and hearts burned, and men knelt to pray, and give thanks to God.

John Ad-ams said the Fourth of Ju-ly ought to be kept up with great pomp through-out A-mer-i-ca,—"with shows, games, sports, guns, bells, and bon-fires"—till the end of time.

The news did not reach New York till Ju-ly 9, and at six o'clock that night Wash-ing-ton read the Act to his troops.

New York was wild with joy, and felt that more must be done than just to ring bells and light fires.

In Bow-ling Green, in front of the fort, there stood a cast of George Third, made of lead. This a mob of men pulled down and broke up, that the lead might be run in-to small shot and be used in the cause for which they fought. This did not please Wash-ing-ton, and he told his troops that they must not take part in such deeds.

The joy did not last long, for on Ju-ly 12, the ships-of-war in the bay sent out a broad-side, and it was thought they would at once fire the town. Crowds were on the streets. The troops flocked to their posts. Fear was in each heart, and New York was in a great stir. But two ships—the *Phoenix* and the *Rose*—left the fleet and shaped their course up the Hudson.

Then the guns were still, and fear died out for a-while. That night there was a fresh scare. Guns boomed and clouds of smoke were seen near the ships-of-war down the bay.

Men on the look-out told that a ship-of-the-line had come in from sea, and each man-of-war gave her a round of guns as she passed by. At her fore-top mast-head she bore the flag of St. George. No need to tell more. "Lord Howe is come! Lord Howe is come!" was the cry that went from mouth to mouth, and the word soon flew through the town, and all felt that the hour of doom was close at hand.

Lord Howe sought peace, and not blood-shed, and hoped, by the terms he would make, to bring not a few hearts back to their King. But he came too late.

The King's troops did not think much of the rank that was borne by our men, who, they felt, had no right to put on the airs they did, and call them-selves grand names.

In a few days Lord Howe sent one of his men on shore with a flag of truce, to seek speech with Wash-ing-ton. The man's name was Brown. His boat was met half-way by a barge which had on board one of our troops, named Reed, to whom Brown said he had a note for *Mis-ter* Wash-ing-ton.

Reed said that he knew no man of that name.

Brown held out to him the note he had in his hand, which bore on its face: *George Wash-ing-ton, Esq.*

Reed said that he could not take the note. He knew what was due to his chief. So there was naught for Brown to do but to take to his oars. He had not gone far when he came back to ask, "What style should be used to please Gen—(here he caught him-self and said) *Mis-ter* Wash-ington. Reed told him that Wash-ing-ton's rank was well known, and Lord Howe could be at no loss as to the right style.

In a day or two an aide-de-camp came with a flag from Lord Howe, and asked if Col-o-nel Pat-ter-son might have speech with *Gen-er-al* Wash-ing-ton. Reed, who met the aide, was prompt to grant this, and pledged him-self that no harm should come to him who came in the King's name.

So the next day Pat-ter-son came, and when he stood face to face with Wash-ing-ton, bowed and said *"Your Ex-cel-len-cy."* Wash-ing-ton met him with much form and state. He was not a vain man, but was proud of the rank he held, and thought that no man— were he a king—had a right to look down on A-mer-i-ca, or show the least slight to her Com-mand-er-in-chief.

When he came to hear the terms on which Lord Howe sought to make peace, he found they were not such as he could take, so the war went on.

CHAPTER X

IN AND NEAR NEW YORK

The red-coats had a camp on Stat-en Isl-and, and for the next month or so ships-of-war came that far up the bay, and brought with them a large force of troops. North-east of them was the long stretch of land known as Long Isl-and, where they could land their troops with ease, and make their way to New York.

Wash-ing-ton knew that he could not keep them back, but he meant to vex them all he could. Gen-er-al Greene was placed with a large force on Brook-lyn Heights, to guard the shore, and troops were sent a mile back to throw up earth-works to check the march of the foe if they should try to come up on the land side.

At mid-night of Au-gust 21, a spy brought word that the King's troops were on the move, and would soon show their strength, and "put all to the sword."

The next day the sound of great guns was heard, and a cloud of smoke was seen to rise from the groves on the south side of Long Isl-and. Word soon came to New York that the King's troops were at Graves-end, and that our troops had fled and set fire to the stacks of wheat to keep them out of the hands of the foe.

Wash-ing-ton at once sent off a large force to check the foe at Brook-lyn, and to lend aid to those in the fort on the Heights. He told them to be cool, but firm; not to fire when the foe were a long way off, but to wait till they were so near that each shot would tell. And if one of them should skulk, or lie down, or leave his place in the ranks, he was to be shot down at once.

Sir Hen-ry Clin-ton led the King's troops, and Lord Corn-wal-lis had charge of the field-guns. Corn-wal-lis made haste to seize a pass that ran through the hills, but found Col-o-nel Hand there with a fine lot of marks-men, and so made a halt at Flat-bush.

This was so near New York that great fright spread through the town. Those who had the means left the place. There was good cause for fear, as it had been told that if our troops had to leave New York it would at once be set on fire. This was false, but they did not know it. Their hearts were full of dread.

Gen-er-al Put-nam was sent to take the place of Gen-er-al Greene who was sick in bed. The brave man was glad when he had leave to go, for he did not want to be kept in New York when there was a chance to fight for the land he loved.

It was nine o'clock on the night of Oc-to-ber 26, that Sir Hen-ry Clin-ton set out with his van-guard, on his march from Flat-bush. Lord Corn-wal-lis brought up the rear-guard with all the large guns, and the large force of troops led by Gen-er-al Howe.

Not a drum was heard, nor the sound of a trump as they took their course through by-roads and on cause-ways till they came near the pass through the Bed-ford Hills where they made a halt.

No guard had been put on the road or the pass by Gen-er-al Greene, who must have thought it too far out of the way to need such care.

Clin-ton was quick to see this, and at the first break of day his troops were on the Heights, and with-in three miles of Bed-ford.

In the mean-time scouts had brought word to our lines that the foe were in force on the right, and Put-nam at once sent out troops to hold them in check.

At day-light small fights took place here and there. A brisk fire was kept up at Flat-bush. Now was heard the big boom of a large field-piece. Then a ship-of-war would send forth a broad-side on the fort at Red Hook. Wash-ing-ton was still in doubt if this was part of the main fight in which New York was to share. Five ships of the line tried to beat up the bay, but were kept back by a strong head wind. As the day wore on, and there were no signs that the red-coats meant to strike New York, Wash-ing-ton went to Brook-lyn in his barge, and rode with all speed to the Heights. He was just in time to see the fight in the woods, which he could do naught to stay.

He stood on a hill, and through his large spy-glass had a view of the whole field. He saw his men cut their way through a host of foes. He saw them caught in traps, and hemmed in so that they were 'twixt two fires.

The whole pass was a scene of blood, and through it rang the clash of arms, the tramp of steeds, the storm of shot, and the cries of men who fought for their lives. On this side and that, our troops were swept down or put to rout by a force they had not strength to meet. Wash-ing-ton wrung his hands at the sight. "Good God!" he cried, "what brave men I must this day lose!"

The red-coats went in-to camp that night in front of our lines, but out of reach of the guns of the fort.

Our loss was 3,000.

Theirs less than 400.

The next day New York Bay and the small isles were wrapped in a dense fog, from which New York was quite free. Here was a chance for the troops to leave the works on the Heights, and make their way to New York.

Fresh troops were sent down from Fort Wash-ing-ton and King's Bridge, and Wash-ing-ton felt that no time should be lost. His fear was that the King's ships would come up the bay at the turn of the tide, sail up the

East Ri-ver and catch in a trap all our troops that were on Long Isl-and.

It was late at night when the troops stole out from the breast works. In the dead of night a big gun went off with a great roar that gave a shock to the nerves of those who were in dread that the least sound might warn the foe of their flight to the New York side.

But no harm came of it, the fog shut out the view, and by day-break our troops had all left the fort and were safe on the New York side. Wash-ing-ton, who had not slept for two days and nights, and had spent most of the time on horse-back, would not step in-to the boat till he saw that all his troops were on board.

The fog rose as the rear boats were in mid-stream, and when the red-coats climbed the crest of the earth-works they found not a sign of life there, and not a thing they could use. Our men had made a clean sweep, and were proud of the way in which they stole a march on the red-coats.

Still, New York was not safe; and Wash-ing-ton sought in all ways to find out the plans of the foe. Ships-of-war went up the Sound, and up the

Hud-son, and guns were fired on the forts that lay on each side of the town. But he knew that if the red-coats took New York they would soon be made to give it up, and so he made up his mind that his best course was to with-draw his troops to Har-lem Heights. This was done, with the loss of a few men who had a fight with some red-coats on the way, and there he stayed a few days, and spent much time on horse-back.

He took note of the land, and chose sites for forts, and breast works, and on Oc-to-ber 23, took his stand at White Plains, where a strong fort was built.

Soon the din of war was heard. The guns from Fort Wash-ing-ton and Fort Lee poured their fire on the men-of-war, but could not keep them back, and the red-coats still gave chase to our troops. Fort Wash-ing-ton fell in-to the hands of the foe in spite of a strong fight made to hold it.

One day Wash-ing-ton went out with some of his staff to look at a height at the north where it was thought he might make a stand, and leave the camp where he then was.

One of them said, "There is the ground where we ought to be."

"Let us go then and view it," said Wash-ing-ton.

They were on their way to the place when a horse-man rode up in haste and cried out, "The red-coats are in camp, Sir!"

"Then," said Wash-ing-ton, "we have some-thing else to do than this," and at once put spurs to his horse and set off for the camp at full speed.

When he reached there he found all his troops drawn up to meet the foe that was close at hand. In his calm way he turned to those who had been out with him on the hills, and said, "Go back to your posts, and do the best you can."

A short, sharp fight took place, in which our troops made a brave stand, but the red-coats were too strong for them, and drove them back to their camp, and seized the hill on which they had stood.

That night the troops of Wash-ing-ton and Howe lay not far a-part. Wash-ing-ton kept his men at work, and forts were built, and earth-works thrown up. These works were made of the stalks of corn, or maize, which the men took from a field near at hand. The roots of the stalks, with the earth on them, were placed on the face of the works, in the same way that sods of grass, and logs of wood were used. The tops were turned in, and loose earth thrown on them so that they were held in place, and made a good shield from the fire of small-arms.

The next day, when Howe saw how much had been done by our troops to add to their strength, he made a change in his plans. His own men were in a sad plight, and not fit to cope with the well-fed troops that kept them at bay. The nights were cold, the Fall rains set in, and not a few of the red-coats were ill. Their chiefs knew how to fight in straight lines, but were not so shrewd and so quick to make use of what lay at hand as our chiefs were. So he broke up his camp, and in a few days the whole force of red-coats fell back from White Plains.

But the strife was kept up at the North, and the foes were at work on sea and on land from New York to Al-ba-ny. Our troops met with ill-luck, and Wash-ing-ton was filled with grief.

Fort Wash-ing-ton was in the hands of the foe; Fort Lee was of no use; and the next move of the red-coats was to cross the Hud-son, north of Fort Lee, and make their way through New Jer-sey. By that means they could shut in all our troops 'twixt the Hud-son and the Hack-en-sack.

Wash-ing-ton at once sent off his men to save the bridge at Hack-en-sack. No time was to be lost. They left the camp with all haste, but ere they could reach the Hack-en-sack the van-guard of the foe was close at their heels. It was thought that a fight would take place, but Corn-wal-lis turned back and some of his troops slept that night in the tents that our men had left.

These were dark days. Wash-ing-ton led his troops through New Jer-sey, hard pressed by Corn-wal-lis, whose van-guard came in-to New-ark just as Wash-ing-ton's rear-guard had left it. His whole camp was in flight. He stayed a few days at New Bruns-wick, in hopes that fresh troops would be sent to his aid, but none came, though his needs were so great. The men who, as he thought, would seize their guns and join his ranks, fled from their homes and sought a safe place as soon as they heard that the red-coats were near.

On De-cem-ber 2, Wash-ing-ton was at Tren-ton, where he made but a brief halt. Then he crossed the Del-a-ware, and left New Jer-sey in the hands of the foe. If he and his men once got to Phil-a-del-phi-a, they would find troops there with whose aide they might hope to turn back the red-coats so close on their track.

Gen-er-al Lee, who was at the heels of the foe, was at Mor-ris-town, De-cem-ber 11, where his troops had been forced to halt for two days for want of shoes. He was a man who loved his ease, and to lie late in bed.

One day as he sat at a desk with pen in hand, one of his aides named Wil-kin-son, who was with him, looked down the lane that led from the house to the main road and saw a band of red-coats on horse-back.

He cried out to Lee, "Here are the red-coats!"

"Where?" said Lee.

"Round the house!"

"Where is the guard?" said Lee with an oath. Where is the guard? Why don't they fire?"

The guards had not thought it worth while to keep watch, when their chief was so much at his ease, so they had stacked their arms and sat down on the south side of a house to sun them-selves. As the horse-men came up they gave chase to the guards who fled for their lives, and left Lee and his aide to do the best that they could.

The red-coats drew near the house where Lee was, and swore that they would set fire to it if the Gen-er-al showed fight. So he was forced to yield, and was brought out in great haste—for they wished to make sure of their prize—and placed on Wil-kin-son's horse which stood at the door. He was but half dressed, had no hat on his head, and wore low shoes, and a loose rough coat. In this style he had to ride to New Bruns-wick, where the King's troops at sight of him set off their big guns, for their joy was great.

The loss of Lee was thought at the time to be a great blow to our cause, as it was hoped that he would do much to bring the war to an end, and to lead the troops out of their sore straits.

In the mean-time Wash-ing-ton was on his way to cross the Del-a-ware.

There was snow on the ground, and the march of the troops could be traced by the blood-spots from the feet of those whose shoes were worn out.

The red-coats were in force at Tren-ton in charge of a man named Rahl, who had done brave work for King George at White Plains and Fort Wash-ing-ton.

Wash-ing-ton's plan was to add to his force, and, as soon as he could, cross the Del-a-ware and strive to wrest Tren-ton from the hands of the foe. He and his force were to cross the stream nine miles north of the town; Gen-er-al Ew-ing was to cross with his troops a mile south of the town; and Gen-er-al Put-nam to leave at a point south of Burl-ing-ton.

It was a bold scheme, full of risk to all who took part in it, yet there was naught to be done but to push on, and hope for the best.

CHAPTER XI

A SAD YEAR

Christ-mas night was the time set to cross the Del-a-ware, and at sun-set the troops were on the move. It was a dark, cold night. The wind was high, the tide strong, and the stream full of cakes of ice which drove the boats out of their course. It seemed at times as if the boats would be crushed to bits. Men who were used to boats, and had been brought up on the sea, and had fought with fierce storms and wild gales, found it hard work, with all their skill, to make their way from shore to shore.

Wash-ing-ton, who crossed with the troops, stood on the east bank till all the field-guns were brought to land, and it was four o'clock ere the men took up their line of march. Tren-ton was nine miles off, and they could not reach there till day-light, too late to take the King's troops off their guard.

Most of the troops at Tren-ton were Hes-sians, from Hes-se, a small Ger-man state whose prince had lent his troops to King George for hire. As

I have told you, they were in charge of Rahl. Rahl thought more of his brass band than he did of his men, was full of good cheer and liked to have a good time. He would sit up till a late hour in the night, and then lie in bed till nine o'clock the next day.

The one who leads troops to war should be like a watch-dog, quick to see and to hear all that goes on, and to be on guard at all times.

Each day he had the guns drawn out and dragged through the town, just to make a stir and have the band out. But when the Ma-jor told him that he should have earth-works thrown up on which to place the guns he said, "Pooh! pooh! Let the foe come on! We'll charge on them with the bay-o-net!"

"But Herr Col-o-nel," said the old Ma-jor, "it costs not much, and if it does not help it will not harm."

But Rahl laughed as if he thought it a good joke, turned on his heel and went off, and the works were not thrown up.

On this night, too, there was a great stir in the camp at Tren-ton, for the men did their best to keep Christ-mas, and their thoughts were of home and the dear ones there. They made what cheer they could, and did not dream that the foe was so near.

A storm of hail and snow set in as soon as our troops took up their march. They could scarce see their way through the sleet they had to face. The night was so cold that two of the men froze to death. At dawn of day some of the men came to a halt at a cross-road, where they did their best to dry their guns. But some were past use, and word was sent to Wash-ing-ton of the state of their arms. They were in doubt what to do.

Wash-ing-ton in a burst of rage bade the man go back to his chief at once, and tell him to push on and charge if he could not fire.

At eight o'clock Wash-ing-ton drew near the town at the head of his troops. He went up to a man who had come out to chop wood by the road-side and asked him where the guard was who stood at the out-post of Rahl's camp.

The man said in a harsh voice, "I don't know."

"You may tell him," said one of our men who stood near, "for that is Gen-er-al Wash-ing-ton."

At once a great change came o'er the man to whom Wash-ing-ton spoke. He raised his hands, and cried, "God bless you! God bless you!" and then showed where the guards could be found.

Soon was heard the cry from Rahl's men, "The foe! the foe! turn out! turn out!" Drums beat to arms. The whole place was in a stir. Wash-ing-ton came in on the north, Sul-li-van on the west, and Stark at the south end of the town.

Rahl scarce knew how to act. He rode to the front of his troops and got them out of the town. Then he seemed to feel that it was a shame to fly in that way, for he was a brave man, so he led his men back in a wild dash out of the woods and in-to the town to meet the foe.

In the midst of the fight, a shot struck him and he fell from his horse. The troops would heed no voice but their chief's, and fled up the banks of a creek on the way to Princeton.

Wash-ing-ton saw the stir and thought they had wheeled to form a new line. He was told that they had laid down their arms, and his joy was great. The day was ours!

But for the wild flight of Rahl's men, it would have gone hard with our troops. Wash-ing-ton did not know it at the time, but he found out that Ew-ing and Put-nam had tried to cross the stream but were kept back by the ice, and he with his raw troops would, he was sure, have been put to rout had Rahl and his men been on their guard.

The poor Ma-jor, who had in vain urged Rahl to throw up breast-works, had a bad wound of which he died in Tren-ton; and Rahl him-self, to whom the red-coats owed their ill-luck, was laid to rest in a grave-yard in that town.

And where was Gen-er-al Howe all this time? In New York, where he thought to take his ease till the Del-a-ware froze so that his troops could cross. He was much shocked at the news that the Hes-sians who had been brought up to war should have laid down their arms for a troop of raw men in rags. He sent Lord Corn-wal-lis back to take Jer-sey, and, as he said, "to bag the fox."

By the third of Jan-u-ary red-coats, with Corn-wal-lis at their head, were near at hand. Wash-ing-ton was in a tight place, with a small creek 'twixt his few raw troops and the large force of the foe. Back of him lay the Del-a-ware which it was now not safe to cross.

In this dark hour a gleam of hope came to his mind. He saw a way out of the trap, and that was by a quick night-march to get at the rear of the King's troops, dash on the camp at Prince-ton, seize the stores that were left there, and push on to New Bruns-wick.

A thaw had set in which made the roads deep with mire, but in the course of the night the wind veered to the north, and in two hours the roads were once more hard and frost-bound.

That the foe might not guess his plan, Wash-ing-ton bade some of his men keep at work with their spades on the pits near the bridge, go the rounds, change guards at each bridge and ford, and keep up the camp-fires till day break, when they were to join those on the way to Prince-ton.

In the dead of the night Wash-ing-ton drew his troops out of camp and the march took place. The road which they had to take was cut through woods, and the stumps of the trees made the march a slow one, so that it was near sun-rise when Wash-ing-ton came to the bridge at the brook three miles from Prince-ton.

As our troops left the woods they came face to face with a force of red-coats, and a sharp fight took place, which did not last long.

Wash-ing-ton was in the midst of it. In the heat of the fight, his aide-de-camp lost sight of him in the dusk and smoke. The young man dropped the reins on the neck of his horse, drew down his cap to hide the tears in his eyes, and gave him up for lost. When he saw Wash-ing-ton come out from the cloud with his hat raised and the foe in flight, he spurred up to his side.

"Thank God you are safe!" cried he.

"A-way, and bring up the troops," said Wash-ing-ton, "the day is our own!"

At day-break, when Gen-er-al Howe thought to bag his fox, he found the prize had slipped from his grasp, and soon learned that the King's troops had lost their hold on New Jer-sey.

The fame of Wash-ing-ton, and of the brave deeds of those who fought to be free, went a-cross the sea, and made friends for him and the cause. Not a few came to their aid. One of these brave souls was a Pole, whose name was Kos-ci-us-ko.

The com-mand-er-in-chief said to him, "What do you seek here?"

"To fight for the cause you have at heart."

"What can you do?"

"Try me."

This style of speech, and the air of the man, pleased Wash-ing-ton so well that he at once made him an aide-de-camp. This was in 1777. He served the cause well, and went back to his own land in 1786 with the rank of Brig-a-dier Gen-er-al.

In 1777 La-fay-ette came from France to join the troops led by Wash-ing-ton. He had wealth and high rank in his own land, and had lived but a score of years. He left his young wife, and the gay court of France, and made his way to A-mer-i-ca to do what he could to aid the foes of King George.

He came, he said, to learn and not to teach, and would serve with-out pay, and as one who came of his own free-will.

He soon won his way to the heart of Wash-ing-ton, and a strong bond of love grew up 'twixt the two which naught but death could break.

In the mean-time the whole of our land south of the Great Lakes was a scene of strife and blood-shed, and it was hard work for our troops to keep the red-skins and red-coats at bay.

I have not space to tell you of all the fights that took place, nor the ways in which Wash-ing-ton sought to vex the King's troops.

On the third of Oc-to-ber of this year—1777—we find him at Ger-man-town, where the main force of the red-coats were in camp. His plan was to drive them out, but though his troops fought with much skill and in the midst of a dense fog, they were forced back, and the day was lost.

The ships-of-war in the Del-a-ware led Wash-ing-ton to think that Lord Howe meant to turn his guns on Phil-a-del-phi-a, and his mind was filled with doubts and fears.

In the same month word came to him that Bur-goyne—who was at the head of the King's troops in the north—had been forced to yield to Gen-er-al Gates at Fish-kill. This was such a blow to the King's cause that the troops at West Point and else-where on the Hudson, who were to have gone to the aid of Bur-goyne, left the forts and made their way to New York.

CHAPTER XII

FOES IN THE CAMP

It is much worse to have one foe in the camp than to have a host of foes out-side, for who can tell what harm he may do who comes in the guise of a friend?

In the year 1774 a young man, named John An-dré, came with the King's troops, and fought in their ranks at St. John's and Crown Point.

He had a brave heart, and a fine mind, and did much to keep up the hearts of the men when in the camp. He was fond of the fair sex and had praised in rhyme the charms of a Miss Ship-pen who wed Ben-e-dict Ar-nold in the year 1780.

Ar-nold had fought well on our side at the north, and won much praise. He had been a sea-man in his youth, and was both strong and brave. But he grew proud and vain, and sought to rank as high as the Com-mand-er-in-chief, with whom he found much fault.

Wash-ing-ton had great faith in him, and did not dream he was false at heart.

For some ill-deeds while at Phil-a-del-phi-a Ar-nold had been brought to court and tried and his guilt proved, and this had made him wroth with Wash-ing-ton, and the cause he had sworn to aid.

He sought for a way to pay back the slight and raise him-self to fame. With this end in view he wrote to Sir Hen-ry Clin-ton—but did not use his own name—that he would like to join the cause of King George on the terms that he set forth. He was in need of funds for he was deep in debt, but Clin-ton did not see fit to make use of him.

Two or three more of his schemes failed, and at last he asked that he might have charge of the post at West Point. This Wash-ing-ton gave him, and in Au-gust Ar-nold fixed him-self in a fine house that stood on the east side of the stream, half a mile or so south of West Point.

From this place he sent notes to An-dré, the aide-de-camp of Clin-ton, who wrote back and signed his name *John An-der-son.*

Ar-nold's plan was to throw West Point and the High-lands in-to the hands of Sir Hen-ry Clin-ton at the time that Wash-ing-ton was at King's Bridge, and the En-glish troops in New York.

A fleet, with a large land force on board, was to come up to the High-lands, and Ar-nold would at once yield up the post in-to their hands. This act he thought would bring the war to an end, with the flag of King George at high mast, and then great would be the name and fame of Ben-e-dict Ar-nold.

That the scheme might not fail, Ar-nold wrote to An-dré to meet him at Dobb's Fer-ry, Sep-tem-ber 11, at noon.

But Ar-nold had spent the night of the 10th at Hav-er-straw, on the west shore, and on his way back in his barge, as he had no flag, he was fired on by the guard boats of the King's troops. So he had to put off his plans for a day or two.

In the mean-time the sloop-of-war, *Vul-ture,* —a good name for such a bird of prey—was brought up the Hudson so as to be near at hand to aid in the vile scheme.

On Sep-tem-ber 18, Wash-ing-ton with his suite crossed the Hud-son at Ver-planck's Point, in Ar-nold's barge, on his way to Hart-ford. Ar-nold went with him as far as Peeks-kill, and talked with him in a frank way, and as if he were most true to the cause.

An-dré went up the Hud-son on the 20th and went on board the *Vul-ture* where he thought to meet Ar-nold. But Ar-nold knew it would not be safe for him to be there; so he kept in the back-ground.

The next night a boat crept up to the side of the *Vul-ture* in which were two men. Their oars scarce made a sound.

An-dré, who wore a blue great coat, went on board this boat and rowed to the west side of the stream. Six miles south of Sto-ny Point they came to shore at the foot of a high mount known as the Long Clove. It was mid-night. Dark was the hour, and dark the place, and dark the deed.

Ar-nold was there hid in the shade of the woods. A man was near who came to wait on him and take care of his horse. He and An-dré had a long talk. One, two, three hours passed, and still there was more to say. One of the men who had brought An-dré, and whose name was Smith, warned them that it was near day-break, and the boat would be seen by our guards if they did not go back soon.

Ar-nold feared that the sight of a boat on its way to the *Vul-ture* might bring harm to him and his scheme, so he urged An-dré to stay on shore till the next night. The boat was sent to a creek up the Hud-son, and An-dré, on the horse that Ar-nold's man had rode, set off with Ar-nold for Smith's house.

The road took them through the small town of Hav-er-straw. As they rode on in the dark the voice of one of the guards at an out-post made An-dré start, for he knew he must be with-in our lines. But it was too late to turn back, and at day-break they reached Smith's house.

Scarce was the door closed on them when the boom of great guns was heard from down the stream. An-dré felt ill at ease, and had good cause for fear.

The fact was that as soon as Liv-ing-ston, who had charge of our troops at Ver-planck's Point, heard that the *Vul-ture* was with-in shot of Tel-ler's Point, which juts out 'twixt Hav-er-straw Bay and Tap-pan Sea, he sent some men and some big guns to that point in the night to fire on the sloop-of-war.

An-dré kept a close watch on the scene from a top room in Smith's house. At one time he thought the *Vul-ture* was on fire; but his heart gave a throb of joy when he saw the sloop-of-war drop down the stream out of reach of gun shot.

Ar-nold gave An-dré the plans of the works at West Point, and told him what and how he was to do. As the *Vul-ture* had changed her place, he told An-dré it would be far more safe for him to go back to New York by land. And he would reach there in less time.

But An-dré said that he must be put on board the sloop-of-war the next night; and in case he should change his mind, Ar-nold gave him a pass that he might go by sea or by land. At ten o'clock that morn Ar-nold left him to his fate.

Time moved at a slow pace with poor An-dré. Once on board the *Vul-ture* he would be safe; his task would be done, and West Point would soon be in the hands of the red-coats. As night set in he grew still more ill at ease, and asked Smith how he had planned to get him on board the *Vulture*.

It gave him a shock to learn that Smith had not done the least thing. The boat-men had gone home, and he would not take him on board the *Vulture*. But he said he would cross the Hud-son with him and start him on the road to New York by land, and go some of the way with him on horse-back.

They set off at sun-set, and went for eight miles on the road to White Plains when they were brought to a halt by a band of our troops who were out as watch-men.

An-dré showed his pass signed with Ar-nold's name, and so they took him for a friend and not a foe. He wore a coat of Smith's that made him look like a plain man.

The two were warned that it was not safe for them to be on the road at night, as they might meet the Cow-Boys from the King's troops, who but a short time since had swept through that part of the land.

Smith was full of fears, and An-dré had to yield to his wish to take a

bed in a farm-house near at hand. This they did, but An-dré could not sleep. He knew that he was not safe. At day-break he woke Smith, and made him haste to leave the place.

Two and a half miles from Pine's Bridge, on the Cro-ton Riv-er, An-dré and Smith took a scant meal at a farm-house which had been stripped by the Cow-Boys.

Here Smith took leave of An-dré, who was to go the rest of the way to New York a-lone. He felt no fear now, as he had passed our lines, and was clear of those who kept watch on the out-posts.

Six miles from Pine's Bridge he came to a fork in the road. The left branch led to White Plains. The right branch led to the Hud-son. He had thought at first that he would take the left hand road, as the right one was said to be filled with Cow-Boys. But he had naught to fear from them, as he was on their side; and as it was a more straight road to New York, he turned down it and took his course on the banks of the Hud-son.

He had not gone far when he came to a place where a small stream crossed the road and ran down a dell that was thick with trees. A man stepped out with a gun and brought An-dré to a stand. Two more armed men came up to aid the first one, whose name was Paul-ding. Paul-ding's coat was in rags, and was of the kind that was worn by the King's troops. When An-dré caught sight of it his heart leaped for joy, for he was sure he was safe. So sure that he did not guard his tongue. He asked the men if they were on his side, and they said they were. He then told who he was, and that he had been sent to a post up the Hud-son and was in haste to get back. As he spoke he drew out a gold watch, such as few owned in those days, and none but men of wealth.

Think what a shock it must have been to An-dré when Paul-ding said they were not his friends but his foes, and he was in their hands.

Then An-dré tried to make out that what he first told was a lie, but that he would now tell the truth; and he drew forth his pass to prove that he was all right. Had he done this in the first place he might have gone on his way. "A still tongue shows a wise head."

The men seized his horse by the rein and told An-dré to get off. He warned them that he had been sent out by Gen-er-al Ar-nold and that they would be ill dealt with if they held him back.

"We care not for that," they said, as they led him through the shrubs on the edge of the brook. They then went to work to search him, and took note of the way in which he was dressed. They were poor men, and had not had a chance to see such fine clothes.

An-dré wore a round hat, a blue great-coat, 'neath which was a red coat decked off with gold-lace, a nan-keen vest, small-clothes and boots.

They made him take off his coat and vest, and found naught to prove that he had sought to harm their cause, and they had a mind to let him go.

Paul-ding, who had been twice in the hands of the red-coats and ill-used by them, was still not quite free from doubt. A thought came to his mind. "Boys," said he, "his boots must come off."

At this An-dré's face flushed, and he said that his boots were hard to get off, and he begged that he might not lose time in this way.

But the men were firm. They made him sit down, his boots were drawn off, and the plans that Ar-nold gave him were brought to light.

Paul-ding looked at them and cried out, "He is a spy!"

He then asked An-dré where he had got these plans. "From a man at Pine Bridge" he said; "a man whom I did not know."

As he put on his clothes An-dré begged the men to let him go. He would pay them a large sum, and stay with two of the men while one went to New York to get it.

Here Paul-ding broke in, "Keep your gold! We want none of it. Were it ten times as much, you should not stir one step!"

An-dré had to yield to his fate, and was led by the men to our post which was ten or twelve miles off. An-dré rode on horse-back with one man in front, and one at each side.

At noon they came to a farm-house, and those who dwelt there sat at the mid-day meal. The house-wife, whose heart was touched by a sight of An-dré's youth and look of grief,

asked him to draw near and take some of the food. Then as she caught sight of his gold-laced coat, the good dame said that she knew it was poor fare for such as he, but it was the best she had.

Poor An-dré shook his head, and said, "Oh, it is all good, but in-deed I can-not eat!"

When the four reached the out-post and Jame-son, who was in charge, saw the plans that had been found on An-dré, he at once saw that they had been drawn up by the hand of Ben-e-dict Ar-nold.

He at once did the thing he ought not to have done, which was to write to Ar-nold, and tell him that a man who said his name was *John An-der-son* had been caught, and held, though he bore a pass signed by him. The plans found on him had been sent to the Com-mand-er-in-chief, and An-dré, with a strong guard was sent with the note to Ar-nold.

In a short time, Ma-jor Tall-madge, who was next in rank to Jame-son, came back from a trip to White Plains. He had a clear head, and as soon as he heard the case he at once urged Jame-son to send a man in haste to bring An-dré back. This was done, but Jame-son had not thought to have the note to Ar-nold brought back, so it sped on to let the knave know that his plot had failed.

As soon as Ar-nold read the note he sprang on the horse of the man who brought it, and rode with all speed to the dock where his six-oared barge lay moored. He threw him-self in-to it and bade his men pull out in mid-stream and row as fast as they could to Tel-ler's Point, as he must be back in time to meet Wash-ing-ton, who was then on his way to West Point.

The guards knew his barge, so they did not fire on it, and a bit of white cloth waved in the air served as a flag of truce. He soon was on board the *Vul-ture,* where he gave him-self up, and the cox-swain and six barge-men with him. This was a mean act, and showed just what kind of a man Ar-nold was, but as soon as the men made it known that they had been led to think that all was right, and that a flag of truce gave them a safe pass, they were at once set free.

Ar-nold gave the red-coats much aid, and they were glad to make use of him. But they did not care to make friends with so base a man. At the close of war, he went to Eng-land, and made his home there. He was shunned by all, and died in the year 1801, at the age of three-score.

As Wash-ing-ton drew near the fort at West Point, he thought it strange that no guns were fired. "Is not Gen-er-al Ar-nold here?" he asked of the man who came down to the shore to meet him.

"No, sir. He has not been here for two days past; nor have I heard from him in that time."

This was strange; but soon the note from Jame-son was placed in his hands, and when he had read of the deep-laid scheme, he said with a deep sigh, "Whom can we trust now?"

Word was at once sent out to the guards to check Ar-nold's flight, but it was too late. He had slipped from their grasp.

Let us now see how An-dré bore his hard fate. He had the best of care, and made hosts of friends, who grieved that one so young, so well-bred, and of such high rank, should have done a crime for which he must be hung.

It was a great grief to Wash-ing-ton, who would have felt no pang had

Ar-nold been in An-dré's place. But death to the spy! was one of the rules of war, and Oc-to-ber 2 was the day set for An-dré to be hung. He had asked that since it was his lot to die he might choose the mode of death; and begged that he might be shot. This Wash-ing-ton could not grant, though in his heart he longed to do so; but thought it best that An-dré should not know.

On the morn of the 2nd, An-dré dressed him-self with great care, in the full suit worn by those who bore his rank in the King's troops. He was calm, while all those near him were in tears.

He walked with a firm step to the place where he was to end his life, arm in arm with two of our troops. When he caught sight of the rope he gave a start, and asked if he was not to be shot. When told that no change could be made, he said, "How hard is my fate!—But it will be but a brief pang!"

Then he stepped in-to the cart, took off his hat and stock, and loosed his shirt at the throat, put the noose round his neck and bound his own eyes.

When told that there was a chance for him to speak if he chose, he said, "I pray you to note that I meet my fate like a brave man."

Then the cart was moved off and he was left in mid-air, and death took place in a short time. An-dré was laid in a grave near the place where he was hung, but in 1821 was borne to the land of his birth, and placed near the tombs of Kings and Queens.

He that breaks laws must pay the price. If you want to make friends, and to have them love and trust you—*be true.* Let no one coax you to sin. The eye of God is on you, and he sees all your deeds. You may hide your crime for a while, but you may *"be sure your sin will find you out."* Be not an Ar-nold nor an An-dré.

CHAPTER XIII

THE HARDSHIPS OF WAR

We will now go back to the place we left, and see where Wash-ing-ton was at the close of the year 1777. He had been forced to leave New Jer-sey in the hands of the King's troops. His own troops were worn down by long and hard toil, and had need of rest. They were in want of clothes too, and could not keep warm in the tents, so he sought out a place where they could build huts and screen them-selves from the cold winds and storms.

He chose Val-ley Forge, which was on the west bank of the Schuyl (school)-kill River, and a score of miles from Phil-a-del-phi-a. Sad was the march of the troops to Val-ley Forge. Food was scant, their clothes were worn out, and a track of blood marked the way they trod. They had fought hard, but not to win, and this made their hearts low.

On De-cem-ber 17, they reached Val-ley Forge, and had to freeze in their tents till they could cut down the trees and build the huts they were to live in. The walls were six feet and a half high, and were made of logs filled in with clay. The roofs were made of logs split in half.

No pen can paint the hard lot of those poor men shut in at Val-ley Forge. For some days they had no meat. For three days they had no bread. Some of the men had to sit up all night by the fires, as there were no clothes for their beds, and they could not sleep for the cold. Some of the men were so scant of clothes that they could not leave their huts.

Wash-ing-ton was kept short of funds and of troops, though he plead hard for both, and was sore pressed on all sides. He scarce knew what to do. There was but one thing he could do, and that was to wait.

While his troops were in this sad plight—some of them sick un-to death—the red-coats, who held Phil-a-del-phi-a in siege, led a gay sort of life, and were much at their ease.

Near the first of March a Ger-man came to Wash-ing-ton's camp to lend him his aid.

His name was Bar-on Steu-ben. He had fought for long years in the wars that had been waged in Eu-rope, had been aide-de-camp to Fred-er-ick the Great, and had won much fame by his brave deeds. The French, who were friends to our cause, knew that we had need of such a man as Bar-on Steu-ben, and urged him to come to A-mer-i-ca, and he was at once sent to join the troops at Val-ley Forge.

Our troops had had no chance to drill, there was no one to teach them, and they fought with a rush and a dash, and in a pell-mell sort of way. Steu-ben went to work to drill these men, the best of whom had much to learn, and he found it a hard task at first as he could not speak our tongue. At last a man was found who spoke French, and him Steu-ben made his aide-de-camp and kept him close at hand.

The men were slow to learn, for the drills were new to them, and Steu-ben would get wroth with them and call them "block-heads," and all sorts of hard names. But though he had a sharp tongue, and was quick to get in a rage, he had a kind, true heart, and soon won the love of the men.

For eight months the red-coats had held Phil-a-del-phi-a. In the spring Gen-er-al Howe went home, and left his troops in charge of Sir Hen-ry Clin-ton, who made up his mind to lead the troops back to New York. But he did not wish his plans to be known.

In the mean-time, Wash-ing-ton knew that a scheme of some sort was on foot—so he sent troops out to check the King's troops should they move by land. The red-coats left Phil-a-del-phi-a on June 18, and as there was but one road for them to take, their train stretched out for twelve miles. They made a halt at Al-len-town, and Clin-ton had not quite made up his mind which way to go from that place. He at first thought he would go as far as the Rar-i-tan Riv-er, and then ship his troops to New York; but when he found that our troops were not far off, he turned to the right and took the road to Mon-mouth.

His march was a slow one; the heat was great; the rains made the roads bad, and they had to stop to bridge the streams, and to build cause-ways so that they could cross the swamps.

Wash-ing-ton in the mean-time had gone on to Kings-ton; but as soon as he learned Clin-ton's course, he moved his troops so as to get in the rear of the red-coats.

On the night of June 27, the foe went in camp on the high ground near Mon-mouth Court House. The van-guard of our troops was five miles off, and in charge of Gen-er-al Lee.

At day-break the van-guard of the red-coats set forth down the hill, while Clin-ton with his choice troops stayed in camp on the heights of Free-hold, to give the long train of carts and pack mules a chance to get well on the way. At eight o'clock all were in line of march to Mid-dle-town.

As soon as Lee heard that the foe were on the move, he set out to meet them, and was joined by the troops in charge of La-fay-ette. As Lee stood on one of the hills he caught sight of a band of red-coats hid some-what by the woods, which he thought was a part of the main force. So he sent some of his troops to draw their fire and check them in the rear, while he with the rest of his force would take a short cut through the woods, get in front of the corps, and cut it off from the main force.

Wash-ing-ton was on his way with his main force, when the boom of big guns rang out on the air. The sound caused him to change his pace to a quick step, and when he drew near Free-hold church, where the road forked, he sent Greene with part of his force to the right, while he with the rest of the troops took the left hand road.

Wash-ing-ton stood on the ground with his arm thrown up on the neck of his horse, when a man rode up and said the blue-coats were in flight. Wash-ing-ton was vexed, for he was quite sure it was not true. Then up came one with fife in hand, quite out of breath, and in great fright. He was seized at once so that he would not scare the troops then on their way and told that he would be flogged if he dared to spread the tale he had brought.

Wash-ing-ton sprang on his horse, and sent men out to learn the truth, while he spurred past the Free-hold church. The news seemed too strange to be true. He had heard but a few guns, and did not think there had been much of a fight. Was Lee to blame for this wrong move? He feared so. As he reached the high ground he saw Lee and his men in full flight, and by this time he was in a fine rage.

"What do you mean by this?" he asked in a fierce stern tone as Lee rode up to him.

At sight of Wash-ing-ton's face Lee was struck dumb for a-while, but when he could speak he tried to tell why he had thought it best to fall back. There was not much time for a talk, as the foe were not far off. The sight of their Com-mand-er-in-chief put a stop to the flight, and plans were at once made to turn the luck. The place where they were was good for a stand, as it was on high ground which the foe could not reach but by a cause-way.

Lee knew that Wash-ing-ton had lost faith in him, so he held back, and would give no aid to his chief. Wash-ing-ton rode back to Lee in a calm mood, and said to him, "Will you keep the com-mand on this height, or not? If you will, I will go back to the main force and have it formed on the next height."

Lee said it was all the same to him where he was placed, that he would do just as Wash-ing-ton said,

and "not be the first to leave the ground."

Soon guns were heard on both sides. Lee and his men, who were in the fore-ground made a brave stand, but were at length forced to fall back. Lee brought off his troops in good style by the cause-way that crossed the swamps, in front of our troops in charge of Lord Stir-ling, and was the last to leave the ground. When he had formed his men in line back of the swamp, he rode up to Wash-ing-ton, and said, "Here, sir, are my troops, what do you wish me to do with them?"

Wash-ing-ton saw that the men were worn out with long tramps, hard fights, and the great heat, so he told Lee to take them to the rear, and call in all those he might meet with who had fled from his ranks.

The foe sought to turn both our flanks, but were checked by a sharp fire, and at length they gave way and fell back to the ground where Lee had been that morn. Here the woods and swamps were on their flanks, and their front could not be reached but by the cause-way. Great as was the risk, Wash-ing-ton made up his mind to charge the foe, and this was his plan: Gen-er-al Poor was to move round on their right, Gen-er-al Wood-ford on the left, while the big field guns should gall them in front. But night set in ere they could act on this plan. Some of the troops had sunk on the ground, and all were in need of rest. Wash-ing-ton told them to lie on their arms just where they chanced to be when it grew dark, as he meant to go on with the fight at dawn of the next day. He lay on his cloak at the foot of a tree, and La-fay-ette lay near him.

At day-break the beat of drums roused them from their sleep, but the foe had fled, and had been so long on the way that Wash-ing-ton could not hope to check them.

Our loss in the fight at Mon-mouth was 69, while 250 of the King's troops were left dead on the field. Some of the troops on both sides had died in the swamp, and some were found on the edge of a stream that ran through it, where, worn out with their toils, and weak from heat and thirst they had crawled to drink and die.

Lee's pride had been so hurt that he wrote to Wash-ing-ton in a way that he should not have done to his Com-mand-er-in-chief, and he was brought to court by the Board of War and tried for his wrong deeds. His guilt was proved, and he was told that he could not serve for the next twelve months. He went to his home in Vir-gin-i-a where he led a queer kind of a life. His house was a mere shell, and had but one room, but lines were chalked on the floor and each space was used as if it was a room by it-self. Here was his bed, there were his books; in this space he kept all his horse gear, and in that one he cooked and ate his meals.

With pen and with tongue he strove to harm Wash-ing-ton, whom his shafts failed to hurt, and who spoke not an ill word of Lee. He liked him as a friend but did not think he was fit to lead troops to war. Lee died in the course of four years, and on his death-bed he thought he was on the field of war, and his last words were a call to his men to stand by him.

For a year or two more the strife was kept up on the coast from Maine to Flor-i-da, and both red-coats and red-skins took part in scenes that chill the blood to read of. Houses were burned and land laid waste, forts were stormed and seized from our troops whose force was too small to hold them. Now and then there was a gain for our side, but in spite of his ill luck Wash-ing-ton held on with a brave heart, and would die at his post but would not yield.

In the first part of the year 1780 we find Wash-ing-ton in camp at Mor-ris-town, with a host of half-fed and half-clad troops.

No such cold had been known in this zone. The Bay of New York froze so hard that the ships-of-war that lay in it were ice-bound. Food was scant, and there was a lack of fire-wood.

Wash-ing-ton saw what a chance there was for a bold stroke, but he had no funds with which to fit out his troops, or to move them to the coast. The cost of war was great, and gold was scarce. He could not strike a big blow for New York to wrest it from the hands of the foe, as he might have done at this time had his troops been well-fed and well-clad but he would do what he could in a small way.

A bridge of ice had formed 'twixt New Jer-sey and Stat-en Is-land, so Wash-ing-ton sent Lord Stir-ling with 2,500 men to start up and seize a force of 1,200 red-coats. His lord-ship crossed in the night, but was seen and had to fall back to E-liz-a-beth-town. Some of his men fell in-to the hands of the King's troops, and some in-to the hands of Jack Frost.

This raid gave a start to the foe and they set out to tease and vex our out-posts, which they thought could be done at small risk, as there was snow on the ground, and the troops could be borne on sleighs.

Not far from White Plains—and a score of miles from the out-posts of the red-coats—300 of our men had a post in a stone house known as Young's house, as that was the name of the man who owned it. It faced a road which ran north and south down through a rich plain, and so on to New York. Our men kept a close watch on this road, to stop the red-coats who might seek to pass with food or live-stock. The red-coats made up their mind to break up this nest of blue-birds, and the night of Feb-ru-a-ry 2, was set for the task.

The King's troops set out from King's Bridge, some in sleighs and some on horse-back. The snow was deep, and it was hard for the sleighs to break their way through. The troops at length left them, and marched on foot. They could not bring their field guns with them. Now and then they would come to a place where the snow was more than two feet deep, and they had to take by-ways and cross-roads so as not to get near our out-guards.

The sun rose while they were yet six miles or more from Young's house. This spoiled their plan, but still they kept on. Ere they could reach the house, the news flew like wild-fire that the red-coats were near, and men left their farms and homes to aid those in Young's house. But though they fought well, they had not strength to hold the fort. Not a few were killed. The house was sacked and set on fire, and the red-coats made haste to get back to their lines with those of our men whom they had seized, and who were sent to New York and put in the vile jails there.

In the year 1780, France sent ships-of-war and troops to aid our cause, and to drive the red-coats from New York. The French troops were in charge of Count de Ro-cham-beau, who was told to do just as Wash-ing-ton said; for he was Com-mand-er-in-chief.

Wash-ing-ton's heart gave a throb of joy at this proof of good-will, and his grief was that he had not more troops of his own to join with these that he might push for New York at once. He must wait till the rest of the French troops, then on their way, came to port.

In the mean-time his thoughts were turned to the South, where the red-coats, led by Corn-wal-lis, waged a fierce war. Our troops there were in charge of Gen-er-al Greene, who was full of cheer, and did his best to keep the foe at bay, but with poor luck as his force was small.

But Wash-ing-ton had faith in him; yet such a large force of the King's troops had been sent by sea to aid Corn-wal-lis that Wash-ing-ton feared that Greene would not be safe. So he wrote to La-fay-ette, who was on his way to meet the French fleet that had been sent to Ches-a-peake Bay, to push on and join the troops at the South.

At this time Wash-ing-ton was at a place near West Point, and his whole force on the Hud-son, in May, 1781, was not more than 7,000; half of whom were not fit to take the field.

Here word came to him of feuds at the North, and that the foe were in force on the north side of Cro-ton Riv-er.

Col-o-nel De-lan-cey, who led this raid, held the place that An-dré had filled, and bore the same rank, and De-lan-cey's horse-men were the dread of all those who dwelled in that part of the land. Our troops had an out-post not far from Pine's Bridge, in charge of Col-o-nel Greene of Rhode Isl-and, who had served all through the war.

De-lan-cey set out at night at the head of 100 men on horse-back and 200 on foot. They crossed the Cro-ton at day-break, just as the night-guard had been called off, and bore down on the out-post.

They first went to the farm-house where Col-o-nel Greene and Ma-jor Flagg slept, and put a strong guard round it. Ma-jor Flagg sprang from his bed, threw up the sash, and fired at the foe, but was shot through the head and then hacked with sword cuts and thrusts.

They then burst through the door of Greene's room. He was a man of great strength, and for some time kept the foes at bay with his sword, but at last he fell, for what could one man do in such a fight?

By the time the troops sent out by Wash-ing-ton reached the post, De-lan-cey's men had flown. They tried to take Greene with them, but he died on the way, and they left him at the edge of the woods.

Wash-ing-ton felt sad at heart when he heard of the death of his brave and true friend, Col-o-nel Greene, and the next day he had his corpse brought to the west bank of the Hud-son. Guns were fired to tell that one who had fought well had gone to his rest, and strong men shed tears as he was laid in his grave, for his loss was a source of great grief to all.

CHAPTER XIV

THE CLOSE OF THE WAR

In the month of May, Corn-wal-lis had planned to bring his troops to Pe-ters-burg and strike a blow at La-fay-ette who was near Rich-mond. La-fay-ette fled as soon as he heard that Corn-wal-lis had crossed the James River, for he had but few troops and did not care to bring on a big fight till the men came up who were then on the way to aid him.

Corn-wal-lis thought he could soon catch "the boy"—as he called him— but his youth made him spry, and the red-coats did not get up to him.

On June 10, Gen-er-al Wayne came up with 900 men, to add to La-fay-ette's strength, and this made him change his whole plan. With 4,000 men and Ba-ron Steu-ben he might hope to win in a fight with the red-coats, and he turned his face to the foe. Corn-wal-lis was at that time 'twixt La-fay-ette and Al-be-marle Court House, where stores were kept. The Mar-quis, by a night march through a road that had long been out of use, got in front of the King's troops, and held them in check.

Corn-wal-lis turned back, and marched first to Rich-mond, and then to Will-iams-burg, while La-fay-ette kept close in his rear. Here they had a fierce fight, in which the loss was great on both sides, and the gain but small.

At this time word came to Corn-wal-lis that Wash-ing-ton had borne down on New York and that he must send some of his troops to that town. This would leave him too weak to stay where he was, so on Ju-ly 4 he set out for Ports-mouth.

La-fay-ette gave chase the next day and took post nine miles from his camp. His plan was to fall on the rear-guard, when the main force should have crossed the ford at James-town. But Corn-wal-lis guessed what he meant to do and laid a trap for him. A sharp fight took place, in-to which Wayne threw him-self like a mad-man, but the foe were as ten to one and our troops were forced back to Green Springs.

In Ju-ly La-fay-ette wrote to Wash-ing-ton that Corn-wal-lis had left Ports-mouth by sea, and he thought he was on his way to New York. It was true the troops had gone on board the boats, but though wind and tide were fair they did not sail.

With the French fleet to help him, Wash-ing-ton saw a chance to fight the foe by land and sea, so he turned from New York and marched to Vir-gin-i-a to aid La-fay-ette, who longed to have his chief at the head of his troops but did not know he was so near.

As our war-worn troops went through Phil-a-del-phi-a they were hailed with shouts and cheers from the throngs that filled the streets. They kept step to the sound of the drum and fife, and raised a great cloud of dust, for there had been quite a drought.

The French troops passed through the next day, but not in the same style. They made a halt a mile from the town, where they brushed off their gay white and green clothes, and then marched with a light step to the sound of a fine band. Crowds were on the streets, and bright smiles and loud shouts met these who had come from France to lay down their lives if need be for the cause we had at heart.

When Wash-ing-ton turned his back on New York, Sir Hen-ry Clin-ton sent word to Corn-wal-lis that he would not need the troops he had asked for; so Corn-wal-lis went from Ports-mouth to York-town, where he took his stand.

York-town was a small place on the south side of York Riv-er. The stream at this point was not more than a mile wide, but it was so deep that ships of large size and weight could go through. Here he threw up works on both sides of the stream, which gave him a fine strong-hold, as the banks were high and set out from the main-land. He thought there was no foe near but La-fay-ette, and he had no great fear of one so young.

He felt so safe that he wrote to Clin-ton that he could let him have a large force of men to add strength to New York, where it was thought our troops would strike the next blow.

In the mean-time La-fay-ette threw out troops to the rear, to work with the French fleets that would soon be in Ches-a-peake Bay, and so a net was drawn round Corn-wal-lis at a time when he thought he was most safe.

Wash-ing-ton was at Phil-a-del-phi-a on Sep-tem-ber 5, and at Bal-ti-more three days from that time. He left Bal-ti-more on the ninth, at day-break, with but one of his suite, as he was in haste to reach Mount Ver-non. The rest of his suite rode at their ease, and joined him the next day at noon. It was six years since Wash-ing-ton had seen his old home, and how full of toil and care those years had been! In three days he had to leave the dear old place, and with his guests push on to join La-fay-ette, who was at Will-iams-burg. By Sep-tem-ber 25, the French and our troops were in camp near that town, and at once set to work to get things in train for the next fight.

Corn-wal-lis had built forts on the north and south banks of the stream, and had done all he could to add strength to York-town. Ships-of-war were in front, and boats had been sunk at the mouth of the stream. Field-works were at the rear with big guns on top, and there were long rows of trees that had been cut down and left so that their limbs stuck out and made a fence it would not be safe to climb. At the right and left of York-town were deep dells and creeks, and it was not strange that Corn-wal-lis felt that he was in a sure strong-hold.

Our troops were twelve miles off when they took up their march on Sep-tem-ber 28, and that night they went in camp two miles from York-town. Wash-ing-ton and his staff slept on the ground, his head on the root of a tree. The next morn our troops drew out on each side of Bea-ver Dam Creek, the A-mer-i-cans on the east side and the French on the west. The Count de Grasse, with the main fleet, stayed in Lynn Ha-ven Bay so as to keep off the ships that might come from sea to aid the red-coats.

On the night of the first of Oc-to-ber, our troops threw up two earth-works, on which the red-coats turned their guns at day-light and killed three of the men. While Wash-ing-ton stood near the works a shot struck the ground close by him and threw up a great cloud of dust. One of his staff who stood near was in a great fright, but Wash-ing-ton was calm and showed no signs of fear.

On Oc-to-ber 6, our troops set out to dig the trench that the first line would use in the siege of York-town. So dark was the night, and so still were the men, that the foe did not know of it till day-light. Then they fired on them from the forts, but the men were screened and kept at their work. By the ninth, the trench was dug and the guns fixed to fire at the town.

Wash-ing-ton put the match to the first gun, and a storm of balls and bomb-shells dared Corn-wal-lis to come out and fight. For three or four days the fire was kept up on both sides, and bomb-shells crossed in mid-air, and at night flashed forth like great stars with tails a blaze of light. Our shells did much harm in the town, and to the earth-works of the foe.

The red-hot shot from the French forts north-west of the town reached the King's ships-of-war. The Char-on, a 44 gun ship, and three large boats for troops, were set on fire by them. The flames ran up to the tops of the masts, and as the night was dark the scene was a grand one to the eye, but a sad one to the heart.

On the night of the 11th, a new ditch was dug by the troops led by Bar-on Steu-ben, and for two or three days the foe kept up a fire on the men at work.

At eight o'clock on the night of Oc-to-ber 14, they set out to storm both York-town and the Point on the north bank at the same time.

The van-guard of our troops was led by Al-ex-an-der Ham-il-ton. When at school he wrote to one of his boy friends, "I wish there was a war;" and in 1776, when he was but 19 years of age, he was placed at the head of the men who fired the guns and bomb-shells. The next year he was aide-de-camp to Wash-ing-ton, in whom he found a true and wise friend. With great joy and pride Ham-il-ton led the van in a head-long dash past the trees, which they pushed or pulled down with their own hands, where they could not climb them, and was the first to mount the wall. One of his men knelt so that Ham-il-ton could use him for steps, and the rest of the men got up the best way they could. Not a gun was fired, and the fort fell in-to the hands of our troops with a small loss on both sides.

The French stormed the fort at the Point in as brave a way, but with less speed, and lost more men.

Wash-ing-ton stood on the ground in the grand fort where he could see all that took place. An aide-de-camp near him spoke up and said that he ran a great risk from a chance shot through one of the port-holes. "If you think so," said Wash-ing-ton, "you can step back."

Soon a ball struck the gun in the port-hole, rolled on, and fell at his feet. Gen-er-al Knox seized him by the arm. "My dear Gen-er-al," said he, "we can't spare you yet."

"It is a spent ball," said Wash-ing-ton in a calm voice; "no harm is done."

When each charge was made and both forts were in our hands, he drew a long breath, turned to Knox and said, "The work is done *and well done!*" Then he said to his black man, "Bring me my horse," and rode off to see where next his lines should move, and how the trap could be closed on Corn-wal-lis.

Corn-wal-lis found that he could not hold his forts; no troops had come to his aid, and he would soon have to yield to the foe.

This was too much for his pride, so he made up his mind to leave those

who were sick or had wounds, and fly from York-town. His scheme was to cross the stream at night, fall on the French camp ere day-break, push on with all speed, and force his way to the north and join Sir Hen-ry Clin-ton in New York.

A large part of his troops had crossed the stream on the night of Oc-to-ber 16, and the rest were on their way when a fierce storm of wind and rain drove the boats down the stream. They could not be brought back till day-light and it was then too late for them to move on or to turn back.

The hopes of Lord Corn-wal-lis were at an end, and on the 17th he sent a flag of truce and a note to Wash-ing-ton and asked that his guns might cease their fire for one day so that terms of peace could be drawn up.

Wash-ing-ton feared that in the mean-time troops from New York would reach Corn-wal-lis, so he sent word back that his guns should cease their fire for but two hours. Wash-ing-ton did not like the terms drawn up by Corn-wal-lis, so he made a rough draft of such terms as he would grant. These were sent to Corn-wal-lis on the 19th, and he was forced to sign them,

and in two hours his troops were to march out of the forts.

At noon our troops were drawn up in two lines more than a mile in length; the A-mer-i-cans on the right side of the road, the French on the left. At two o'clock the red-coats passed out with slow steps, and were led to a field where they were to ground their arms. Some of them, in their rage, threw down their guns with such force as to well nigh break them.

On the day that Corn-wal-lis had been forced to lay down his arms at York-town, the large force that was to aid him set sail from New York. They did not reach Ches-a-peake Bay till Oc-to-ber 29, and when they found they were too late, they turned their prows and went back to New York.

The down-fall of Corn-wal-lis was felt to be a death-blow to the war, and great joy was felt through-out the land. Votes of thanks were sent to Wash-ing-ton, to De Ro-cham-beau and De Grasse, and Wash-ing-ton gave high praise to all the troops for the way in which they had fought at the siege of York-town.

From that time the red-coats lost heart, and on No-vem-ber 25, 1783, they marched out of New York, and Wash-ing-ton marched in at the head of his brave men, who had fought and bled and borne all the ills that flesh could bear that the land they loved might be free.

In a few days Wash-ing-ton was called to An-nap-o-lis to meet with those who made the laws, and his chief men who had been with him through all the sad scenes of the war, came to bid him good-bye.

With a heart full of love he said to them, "I can-not come to each of you to take my leave, but shall be glad if each of you will come and take me by the hand." This they did. No one spoke a word. Tears were in all their eyes.

Wash-ing-ton left the room, and went on foot to the boat which lay at the end of what was then and is now White-hall Street. His friends kept close in the rear. When Wash-ing-ton was in his barge he turned, took off his hat, and waved good-bye, and those on shore did the same, and watched the barge till it passed out of their sight.

CHAPTER XV

FIRST IN PEACE

At the close of the war, and of the year 1783, Wash-ing-ton went back to Mount Ver-non. He reached his home to his great joy on the eve of Christ-mas day, and he was in a good state of mind to keep the feast.

"The scene is at last closed," he wrote, "and I am eased of a load of care. I hope to spend the rest of my days in peace."

Mount Ver-non was locked in ice and snow for some time. Wash-ing-ton wrote that he was so used to camp life that he could not help feel when he woke each day that he must hear the drums beat, and must go out to plan or to lead his troops. He was now at his ease, and longed for the spring so that his friends could come to him.

He would not give notes of his life to those who wished to write it up at this time lest it should look vain. "I will leave it to those who are to come to think and say what they please of me," he wrote. "I will not by an act of mine seem to boast of what I have done."

As spring came on, friends flocked to Mount Ver-non, and Wash-ing-ton met them in a frank way. His wife, too, was full of good sense and good cheer. She loved to knit, and had been used all through the war to knit socks for the poor men who were in the ranks.

But as Wash-ing-ton took his rides through his place, he felt the changes there since he had left. Old friends were gone, and the scenes of his youth were no more. La-fay-ette spent a few days with him, and the love he felt for the brave young man was as strong as at first.

He wrote a sad note to him when he was gone which showed what a warm place the young French-man had in his heart. He said, "As you left me, I asked if this were the last sight I should have of you. And though I wished to say 'No,' my fears said 'Yes.' I called to mind the days of my youth and found they had long since fled to come back no more. I must now go down the hill I have climbed all these years. I am blessed with strength, but I come of a short-lived race, and may soon go to the tomb. All these thoughts gave a gloom to the hour in which I parted with you.''

Wash-ing-ton made a trip through some of the states of the West, and saw there was a chance for great trade there, and he wrote much of what he had seen. But his chief joy was in his home and land, where he planted trees and loved to watch them grow. He writes down each month of what he sets out; now it is a choice slip of grape vine from France; or it may be a tree that stays green all the year round. Some of the bushes he set out still stand strong in their growth on the place.

He notes the trees best for shade and which will not hurt the grass. He writes of rides to the Mill Swamp in quest of young elms, ash trees, and white thorn, and of the walks he lays out and the trees and shrubs he plants by them.

A plan of the way in which he laid out his grounds is still kept at Mount Ver-non, and the places are marked on it for the trees and shrubs. He owned five farms, and he kept maps of each.

He read much of soils, the way to raise good crops, and the best style of ploughs and farm tools to use. He rode the first half of the day to see that all went well. When he had dined, he would write till dark if he had no guests.

If friends came he did all he could to make them feel at ease and at home. He was kind, and loved by all. He would not talk much of the war nor of what he had done in it.

He took great care not to talk of his own acts, so that if there had been a guest who did not know the facts, he would not have found out a word from Wash-ing-ton that he was one who had won a great name in the eyes of the world.

Though grave in his looks and ways, he loved to see youth glad and gay. He was fond of parties. There had been parties in camp in the dark days of the war.

Wash-ing-ton, as we have seen, had been fond of the hunt in his youth, and La-fay-ette sent him some hounds from France, so he took up his old sport. But the French hounds did not do well, and he found they could not be trusted.

Ere the war had been long past, it was found that there was need of new laws by which the States should be ruled. The chief men of the land were called to Phil-a-del-phi-a to form them, and Wash-ing-ton went from Mount Ver-non to take part in the work. It was then that the code of laws was drawn up which bears the name of "Con-sti-tu-tion of the U-ni-ted States."

These laws said that the States should be ruled by a Pres-i-dent. The choice for this post fell on Wash-ing-ton, and in the spring of 1788, he bade good-bye to Mount Ver-non and made his way to New York, where he was to take the oath that he would serve the land and be true to her in peace and in war.

As he passed through the towns, crowds came out to cheer him, flags were raised, guns roared, and at night there was a great show of fire-works.

When he came to Tren-ton, the place where in the past he had crossed the stream in the storm, through clouds of snow and drifts of ice, he found a scene of peace and love. Crowds were on the bank, the stream gleamed in the sun, the sky was blue, and all hailed him with joy.

On the bridge that crossed the Del-a-ware, an arch was raised and twined with wreaths of green and gay blooms. As Wash-ing-ton passed 'neath it, a band of young girls, dressed in white and with wreaths on their heads, threw bright blooms at his feet, and sang an ode that spoke the love and praise that were in all hearts.

At Eliz-a-beth-town Point he was met by men who had been sent from New York, and led to a barge which had been made for his use. It was filled with sea-men of high rank, who made a fine show in their white suits.

Boats of all sorts, gay with flags, and some with bands on board, fell in the wake of Wash-ing-ton's barge, and as they swept up the bay of New York the sight was a grand one. The ships at the wharves or in mid-stream, dipped their flags, and fired their guns, bells were rung, and on all the piers were great crowds that made the air ring with their shouts.

On the last day of A-pril, 1789, Wash-ing-ton took the oath in front of the hall where the wise men of the land had been wont to meet in New

York. He stood in full view of a great crowd to whom this was a new and strange sight. The States were to be as one, and this man, whose name and fame were dear to them, was to pledge him-self to keep them so.

On a ledge that bulged out from the main part of the house, was a stand with a rich red cloth on which lay the Word of God, the Book of Books. Wash-ing-ton was clad in a full suit of dark-brown home-made cloth, white silk hose, and dress sword with steel hilt, and his hair was dressed in the style of the day.

As he came in sight he was hailed with the shouts of the crowds in the streets and on the roofs. He came to the front of the ledge close to the rail, so that he could be seen by all, laid his hand on his heart, bowed three or four times, and then went back and took his seat in an arm-chair near the stand.

In a short time he rose and went once more to the front with John Ad-ams, who was to be next him in rank, and the friends who were to stand by him in this new field. While the oath was read Wash-ing-ton stood with his hand on the Word of God, and at the close he said, "I swear—so help me

God!" One of the men would have raised the book to Wash-ing-ton's lips, but he bent his head and kissed it.

Then there was a cry of "Long live George Wash-ing-ton!" and all the bells in the town rang out a peal of joy, and the crowd rent the air with their shouts and cheers.

Wash-ing-ton bowed and made a speech that was full of good sense. Then all went on foot to St. Paul's Church to pray that God would bless the land.

Wash-ing-ton felt most of all as he wrote to his friends, a fear lest he should come short of what the land hoped to find in him. The eyes of the world were on him. He had won fame in the field, but how would he rule the State? There was still much to be done. Great Brit-ain held some of the posts at the West, on the plea that debts due to some of her men had not been paid; the red-men were still a source of fear to the homes in the Wild West; and there was no hard cash with which the States could pay their debts.

He found that his time was no more his own. From dawn till dark men came to him, and he saw that he must be saved from this or he could do no work. Mrs. Wash-ing-ton joined him and soon days were fixed for the calls of friends. The house was kept well, but there was no waste.

One who dined there wrote that there was no show. The Pres-i-dent said a short grace as he sat down. He was kind to his guests and strove to put them at their ease.

He was strict in the way he kept the Lord's day. He went to church and would have no calls on that day.

As to Mrs. Wash-ing-ton, those who knew her at the time speak of her as free from all art. She met her guests in a well-bred way as one who had ruled in a great house. She, too, was more fond of their home at Mount Ver-non than of the new rank and place. To stay at home was the first and most dear wish of her heart.

Wash-ing-ton was touched to the quick when he heard that someone had said that there was more pomp at his house than at St. James, where King George held his court, and that his bows were much too stiff and cold.

Wash-ing-ton wrote, "I grieve that my bows were not to his taste,

for they were the best I can make. I can say with truth that I feel no pride of place, and would be more glad to be at Mount Ver-non with a few friends at my side, than here with men from all the courts of the world." He then goes on to tell how they treat their guests. "At two or three o'clock each Tues-day they come and go. They go in and out of the rooms and chat as they please. When they first come in they speak to me, and I talk with all I can. What pomp there is in all this I do not see!"

The red-men, who could not be kept in peace, roused the land once more to arms. Wash-ing-ton thought it would be a good plan to meet the In-di-an chiefs and talk with them. Three chiefs came to him, and said they would go to the rest and try to make peace. Wash-ing-ton made a set speech and told them it would be a good work to do, or else those tribes, "if they thieved and killed as they had done, would be swept from the face of the earth."

He had thought much of the state of the red-men in the land. He had but small faith in schools for the youth, save as far as to teach them to read and write. The true means to do them good, he thought, was to teach them to till the ground and raise crops in the same way as the white folks, and he said if the tribes were pleased to learn such arts, he would find a way to have them taught.

In the end, Gen-er-al St. Clair had to be sent out with troops to put the red-men down. Wash-ing-ton's last words to him were to be on the watch, for the red-skins were sly and would wait to find him off his guard.

But St. Clair did not pay heed to these wise words, and the red-skins got in-to his camp, some of his best men were slain, and the whole force was put to rout.

When the news was brought to Wash-ing-ton he said in a quick way, "I knew it would be so! Here on this spot I took leave of him and told him to be on his guard! I said to him 'you know how the red-skins fight us!' I warned him—and yet he could let them steal in-to his camp and hack and slay that ar-my!" He threw up his hands, and his frame shook, as he cried out "O what a crime! what a crime!"

Then he grew calm, and said that St. Clair should have a chance to speak, and he would be just to him. St. Clair was tried, and was found free from guilt.

Wash-ing-ton's mo-ther died at Fred-er-icks-burg, Vir-gin-i-a, Au-gust 25, 1789, aged 82. When her son first went to war, she would shake her head and say, "Ah, George should stay at home and take care of his farm." As he rose step by step, and the news of his fame was brought to her, she would say "George was a good boy," and she had no fear but that he would be a good man, and do what was right.

In the year 1789, a great war broke out in France, in which Lou-is XVI lost his crown and his head, and deeds were done that you could scarce read of with-out tears. Men seemed like fiends in their mad rage, and like wild beasts in their thirst for blood.

In 1793 France made war on Eng-land; and in 1797 sought to break up the peace of the Un-i-ted States, but of this I will tell you by and by.

In the mean-time the four years—which was the full term Wash-ing-ton was to rule—came to an end. He had no wish to serve for two terms, but the choice fell on him, and he once more took the oath, on March 4, 1792. In 1796, as France was still at war, it was thought best that Wash-ing-ton should hold his place for a third term.

But this he would not do. He had made up his mind to leave these scenes and to give up that sort of life, and those who plead with him could not move him. He took leave of his friends in a way that moved them to tears; and his fare-well speech, though in plain style, touched all hearts and made them feel what a loss it was to part with so great and good a man.

On March 4, 1797, John Ad-ams took the oath, and bound him-self to serve as Pres-i-dent for a term of four years. Wash-ing-ton was there, and as he rose to leave the house there was a great rush to the door, as all wished to catch the last look of one who had had for so long a time the first place in their hearts. So great was the crush that it was feared there would be loss of limbs if not of life.

As Wash-ing-ton stood in the street he waved his hat as cheer on cheer rose from the crowd, and his gray hairs streamed forth in the wind. When he came to his own door he turned to the throng with a grave face and tried to say a word or two. But tears rose to his eyes, his heart was full, and he could not speak but by signs.

He soon set off for Mount Ver-non, the dear home of his heart. He had been there but a few months when the French, by their acts, seemed to want to bring on a war with the U-ni-ted States. They took our ships at sea, and there was no way left but to stand up for our rights.

Pres-i-dent Ad-ams wrote to Wash-ing-ton, "We must have your name, if you will let us have it. There will be more in it than in a host of men! If the French come here we shall have to march with a quick step."

Wash-ing-ton wrote to Pres-i-dent Ad-ams, "I had no thought that in so short a time I should be called from the shade of Mount Ver-non. But if a foe should come in our land, I would not plead my age or wish to stay at home."

He saw the dark clouds that showed a storm, and he feared his days of peace would be few. It was with a sad heart that he felt his rest was at an end, but he had so strong a sense of what was right that he did not hold back. He said he would do all he could for the troops, but he would not take the field till the foe was at hand.

For months Wash-ing-ton led a life full of hard work. He had much to do for the troops, and at the same time work at home. He would write for hours, and took long rides each day. To his great joy, there was, in the end, no war with France.

He seemed in first-rate health up to De-cem-ber 12, 1799. On that day a storm set in, first of snow, then of hail, and then of rain, and Wash-ing-ton was out in it for at least two hours. When he reached the house his clerk, Mr. Lear, saw that the snow hung from his hair, and asked him if he was not wet through. "No," said Wash-ing-ton, "my great coat kept me dry." But the next day his throat was sore and he was quite hoarse; and though much worse at night he made light of it and thought it would soon pass off.

When he went to bed Mr. Lear asked him if he did not think it best to take some-thing. "Oh, no," said Wash-ing-ton. "Let it go as it came." But he grew worse in the night, and it was hard for him to breathe, and though his wife wished to call up one of the maids he would not let her rise lest she should take cold.

At day-break, when the maid came in to light the fire, she was sent to call Mr. Lear. All was done that could be done to ease him of his pain, but he felt him-self that he had but a short time to live. Mr. Lear was like a son to him, and was with him night and day.

When Mr. Lear would try to raise and turn him so that he could breathe with more ease, Wash-ing-ton would say, "I fear I tire you too much." When Lear told him that he did not, he said, "Well, it is a debt we must all pay, and when you want aid of this kind I hope you'll find it."

His black man had been in the room the whole day and most of the time on his feet, and when Wash-ing-ton took note of it he told him in a kind voice to sit down.

I tell you these things that you may see what a kind heart he had, and how at his last hour he thought not of him-self.

His old friend, Dr. Craik, who stood by his side when he first went forth to war, in the year 1754, was with him in these last hours, when Death was the foe that Wash-ing-ton had to meet. He said to Dr. Craik, "I die hard, but I am not a-fraid to go, my breath can-not last long." He felt his own pulse, and breathed his last on the night of De-cem-ber 14, 1799.

His wife, who sat at the foot of the bed, asked with a firm voice, "Is he gone?" Lear, who could not speak, made a sign that he was no more.

"Tis well," said she in the same voice. "All is now at an end, and I shall soon join him."

Thus lived and died this great and good man, "first in war, first in peace, and first in the hearts of" those who love "the land of the free."

Praise did not spoil him or make him vain; but from first to last he was the same wise, calm, true friend, full of love to God and of good-will to man.

Great and good men have been born in-to the world, but none whose name and fame rank as high as that of GEORGE WASH-ING-TON.